T0329275

THE PARABLES OF THE GOSPELS

A · M · D · G

ET IN MEMORIAM

A · M · H

THE PARABLES OF THE GOSPELS

IN THE LIGHT OF MODERN CRITICISM

HULSEAN PRIZE ESSAY, 1912

by

LAURENCE E. BROWNE, M.A.

Late Scholar of Sidney Sussex College
Lecturer at St Augustine's College, Canterbury

Cambridge:
at the University Press
1913

CAMBRIDGE
UNIVERSITY PRESS

University Printing House, Cambridge CB2 8BS, United Kingdom

Published in the United States of America by Cambridge University Press, New York

Cambridge University Press is part of the University of Cambridge.

It furthers the University's mission by disseminating knowledge in the pursuit of
education, learning and research at the highest international levels of excellence.

www.cambridge.org
Information on this title: www.cambridge.org/9781107665019

© Cambridge University Press 1913

First published 1913
First paperback edition 2014

A catalogue record for this publication is available from the British Library

ISBN 978-1-107-66501-9 Paperback

PREFACE

IN the investigation of the Parables of Jesus the name of Jülicher stands pre-eminent. His work marked a great turning point in their interpretation. It is not without due respect for his learning that exception has been taken to some of the leading principles on which he based his theory. Disagreement with some of his root principles has led to such a complete restatement of the case, that a casual reader might be led to think that the object of this essay was merely to contradict Jülicher on every side. The reality is far from being so. To no writer do we owe so much as to him, chiefly indeed for the masterly way in which he raises the questions, but also for showing to what conclusions one must be led by his premises. Of those who follow him in his theory we should perhaps chiefly mention Weinel, who gives the theory with scarcely any modification in a concise form. For any who might be inclined to doubt the value of Jülicher's work we might quote from a book only published in 1903[1]. Among other reasons for the use of parables the author gives as one that "the parable sets a new value on the truth by making men take pains to find it out." It seems then that Jülicher's pioneer work is needed even to-day to contradict such statements as this which see the

[1] *The Parables of Jesus,* by various authors. Chap. I by G. H. Morrison.

difficulty of parables in their form rather than in their substance. For direct criticism of Jülicher's work we have used Fiebig's book published early in 1912. He approaches the question merely on one side, and his conclusions sometimes seem to go beyond the evidence he brings forward. The rabbinic parables quoted in this essay are all taken from his book. Spitta's articles on the Parable of the Shepherd in the Fourth Gospel have been found most suggestive and useful; while Lagrange's articles in the *Revue Biblique Internationale* contain some of the wisest criticism of the parables that we have seen. A work by Otto Eissfeldt, *Der Maschal im alten Testament,* has appeared too late this year to be made use of.

It is scarcely possible in such a subject as this to say anything really original. Jülicher did not even claim it for his own work. We are all children of our generation, and the most that we can hope for is, here to express a thought more clearly than it has been expressed before, here to rescue some thought that was in danger of oblivion, here to gather together various strands of thought and weave them into a unity.

It has been a great pleasure to me to be able to make even this small contribution to theological study, amidst the engrossing work of a large town parish.

L. E. B.

CANTERBURY.
September, 1913.

CONTENTS

The following are the principal works used :

ADOLF JÜLICHER : "Die Gleichnisreden Jesu," 2 Teile, 1910 (first edition 1888 and 1889).

HEINRICH WEINEL : (1) "Die Gleichnisse Jesu," 3rd edition 1910.
(2) Zeitschrift für die neutestamentliche Wissenschaft, 1912, Heft 2, "Der Talmud, die Gleichnisse Jesu, und die synoptische Frage."

PAUL FIEBIG : "Die Gleichnisreden Jesu im Lichte der rabbinischen Gleichnisse des neutestamentlichen Zeitalters," 1912.

M. J. LAGRANGE : (1) Revue Biblique Internationale, 1909, pp. 198 and 342, "La parabole en dehors de l'Évangile."
(2) R. B. I. 1910, p. 5, "Le but des paraboles d'après l'Évangile selon Saint Marc."

F. C. BURKITT : The Interpreter, Jan. and July 1911, "The Parables of the Kingdom of Heaven."

B. H. STREETER : The Interpreter, Apr. 1911, "Prof. Burkitt and the Parables of the Kingdom."

JAMES DENNEY : The Expositor, Aug. and Sept. 1911, "Criticism and the Parables."

FRIEDRICH SPITTA : Zeitschrift für die neutestamentliche Wissenschaft, 1909, Hefte 1 and 2, "Die Hirtengleichnisse des vierten Evangeliums."

CHAPTER I

SIMILITUDE AND ALLEGORY

The first question that a child asks on being told a tale is "Is it true?" In the same way the first enquiry to which we are tempted as we begin to deal with the parables of the Gospels is their genuineness. It is of the utmost importance to the child to know whether Hänsel and Gretel, Romulus and Remus, Adam and Eve, really lived; and yet the impatience for an answer must often be checked until the child is older. For us too the question of the authenticity of the parables, although it is so important, must wait awhile for an answer. It is not to be judged on external evidence alone, but on the internal evidence of the parables themselves. We must therefore first set ourselves to find out the nature and *raison d'être* of these stories which fill so large a part of the Gospels. In other words, What is a parable?

The uses of the Hebrew and Greek words for a parable do not, as we shall see later, give us any immediate help, for they include a variety of figures of speech. Broadly speaking they include any kind of speech that was thrown into figurative or pictorial form.

Now there are two kinds of figurative speech to be sharply distinguished, Allegory and Similitude[1]. In their simplest form they are called respectively Metaphor and Simile. In Metaphor a word in the sentence to be expressed is replaced by a word denoting an object in some respect similar; frequently it is an abstract word which is replaced by a concrete. Eph. vi. 11 says " Put on the whole armour of God " meaning " Put on the whole protection (or defence) of God," the word 'armour' of concrete meaning replacing the abstract word 'protection.' In Simile on the other hand the abstract action is explained by comparison with a concrete action; e.g. it is simile to say (Ps. v. 12) " O Lord, thou wilt compass him with favour as with a shield."

In Allegory the exchange of one term for another which takes place in Metaphor is repeated, so that an allegory might be described as a string of metaphors. The metaphors are not chosen at random and strung loosely together, but are all taken from one sphere, so forming a connected whole. As an example let us take the well-known allegory of Jotham in Judges ix. 8–20:

[1] I use the word Similitude as equivalent to *Gleichnis*, keeping the word Parable, in a less restricted sense, for the parables of Jesus, and similar stories.

" The trees went forth on a time to anoint a king over them ; and they said unto the olive tree, Reign thou over us. But the olive tree said unto them, Should I leave my fatness, wherewith by me they honour God and man, and go to be promoted over the trees ? And the trees said to the fig tree, Come thou, and reign over us. But the fig tree said unto them, Should I forsake my sweetness, and my good fruit, and go to be promoted over the trees ? Then said the trees unto the vine, Come thou, and reign over us. And the vine said unto them, Should I leave my wine, which cheereth God and man, and go to be promoted over the trees ? Then said all the trees unto the bramble, Come thou, and reign over us. And the bramble said unto the trees, If in truth ye anoint me king over you, then come and put your trust in my shadow : and if not, let fire come out of the bramble, and devour the cedars of Lebanon. Now therefore, if ye have done truly and sincerely, in that ye have made Abimelech king, and if ye have dealt well with Jerubbaal and his house.... then rejoice ye in Abimelech, and let him also rejoice in you. But if not, let fire come out from Abimelech, and devour the men of Shechem, and the house of Millo."

Here we are given to understand that the word ' bramble ' is put for ' Abimelech,' the word ' trees ' for ' men of Shechem,' the ' olive,' ' fig ' and ' vine ' for other great men who might have been rulers over Shechem, the ' fatness,' etc. is the utility in some direction other than the mere holding sway, and the ' fire ' from the bramble is the destruction by Abimelech of those who do not trust and obey him. This string of metaphors constitutes an allegory. All the metaphorical terms used belong to the sphere of plant life, thus giving coherence to the collection of metaphors. Although then the story as it stands is outside the range of possibility, yet it can be imagined and is therefore interesting. In order to get the meaning that Jotham wished to convey it is only necessary to exchange the words as explained above. No alteration has to be made in the relations between the different elements in the story: those relations are not similar to, but the same as, those intended to be understood. It is this fact indeed which makes the story as it stands impossible because they happen to be relations which do not obtain in the case of trees. By most authors figurative speech in which plants and animals play the chief parts is called fable, implying the impossibility of the story. But for our purpose this distinction is of no importance, and is best avoided. What is important to us is whether the speech is of the nature of similitude or allegory.

Take as another example of allegory an ancient hymn:

> "Christian, dost thou see them
> On the holy ground,
> How the troops of Midian
> Prowl and prowl around?"

This is an extremely simple allegory. In order to get the required meaning it is only necessary to read 'spirits tempting to evil' for 'troops of Midian,' and perhaps 'seat of the soul' for 'holy ground.' All the relationships are written word for word as intended to be understood.

In general words, it is allegorising when a man wishes to tell something about certain elements A, B, C, D, etc., and writes down instead of them a, b, c, d, etc., only fitting them into the same relations that exist between A, B, C, etc. There is a similarity of some kind between each pair, so that one may say that the values $\frac{A}{a}$, $\frac{B}{b}$, $\frac{C}{c}$, etc. are known quantities. This is well seen in the examples given above.

In Simile and Similitude on the other hand the comparison is not between one element and another but between one relationship and another. A simple example is Ps. xlii. 1:

> "Like as the hart desireth the water-brooks,
> So longeth my soul after Thee, O God!"

where the one relationship compared is the desire of a hart for water with the longing of the soul for God. This may be expanded with greater detail without there being any further relation to be compared:

> "As pants the hart for cooling streams,
> When heated in the chase,
> So longs my soul, O God, for Thee,
> And Thy refreshing grace."

The one relation compared is the same as before; nor would it need great ingenuity to construct quite a long story about a hart which after many adventures succeeded in reaching a stream for refreshment, without bringing in more than this one relation of the longing

of the soul for God. But now Jülicher asserts that
however much a similitude be embellished there is
never more than one relation to be compared[1]. According to him the speaker wishes to convey a judgment or decision (*Urteil*) on some matter, and in order
to do so tells the similitude in which the same judgment is obvious. So far that is often true, for,
especially in similitudes of an argumentative kind—as
opposed to such as are merely explanatory—the main
object is to bring out a judgment. But this one
judgment may result from a comparison of a number of
relationships. To illustrate this idea of several relationships compared, with the object of bringing out one
judgment, let us consider Rabbi Akiba's Similitude of
the Fox and the Fishes[2]:

"Once the evil kingship ordered the Israelites not to busy
themselves with the Law. Pappus ben Jehudah came and met
Rabbi Akiba holding an assembly in the street, and busying
himself with the Law. He said to him, 'Akiba, fearest thou not
the evil kingship?' He replied, 'I will tell thee a parable.
What is the matter like? It is like a fox who went along the
bank of a river and saw fishes which gathered together from one
place to another. He said to them, "Why do ye flee away?"
They said to him, "Because of the nets which men bring over

[1] Jülicher, *Die Gleichnisreden Jesu*, 1 Teil, p. 317: "die
Parabel ist immer nur da, jenen einen Punkt, ein Gesetz, eine
Idee, eine Erfahrung, die im geistlichen wie im irdischen Leben
gilt, zu beleuchten."

[2] I translate from Fiebig's German, *Die Gleichnisreden Jesu*,
p. 79.

us." He said to them, "Were it your will to mount up on to dry land we might dwell, ye and I, as my fathers dwelt with your fathers." They said to him, "Art thou he of whom it is said that he is the cleverest of beasts? Thou art not clever but rather foolish. If we are already afraid in the place of our life (i.e. in the water), how much more in the place of our death (i.e. on dry land)?" So we too: if we fear now where we sit and busy ourselves with the Law, in which it stands written, "For that is thy life and the length of thy days" (Deut. xxx. 20), how much more if we go off and are neglectful of it?'"

The one judgment to which the hearer is forced is that as it was the wisest course for the fishes to remain in their natural sphere, the water, so it is the wisest course for the Jew to remain in *his* natural sphere, the study of the Law. But it would be quite wrong to suppose that only one relationship is compared. To begin with fishes living in the water, their natural home, are compared with Jews living in the study of the Law. Then fishes stranded on dry land are compared with Jews trying to live without the Law. Further the men trying to catch the fish are compared with the evil kingship trying to prevent the Jews from living in the Law; and the fox giving stupid advice is probably compared with Pappus ben Jehudah whose advice is equally foolish. We have three or four relationships compared. The story is therefore parallel to the matter to be expressed, not as Jülicher would assert in one point only, but in three or four. Such a close parallelising as this Jülicher would call allegorising, but yet these examples of similitude lack

the one essential of allegory, which is that elements
(not relationships) in the picture-story shall be related
in some way to the corresponding elements in the
matter expressed[1]. For instance there is no relationship between a hart and the soul, between water-brooks
and God, between fish and Jews, a river and the Law,
and so on. Writing it as we did in the case of allegory:
we wish to express the relationships between elements
A, B, C, D, etc., and we tell the relationships between
other elements a, b, c, d, etc. But $\dfrac{A}{a}$, $\dfrac{B}{b}$, $\dfrac{C}{c}$ are not
known quantities, since there is no point in A by which
it can be compared with a. In a similitude we are
told that $A:B:C:D = a:b:c:d$. A common illustra-
tion will make this clearer. We wish to express in the
concrete the abstract passing of time. The elements
we wish to express are the intervals when 1 min.,
2 min., 3 min., etc. have passed. We express it in the
concrete by the movement of a minute hand through
angles of 6°, 12°, 18°, etc. The angular movement of
the minute hand is a similitude of the passing of time.

---

[1] They do not in fact go beyond the dictum of Maldonatus
(ad Matth. xi. 16): "Nunc satis est ut moneamus ualde esse
usitatum ut in parabolis non personae personis, non partes
partibus, sed totum negotium toti negotio comparetur….Itaque
frustra laborat, qui anxie quaerit quomodo personae personis
partes partibus respondeant, totum sententiae corpus intuendum
est, et integrum ex integra parabola tradendum : ne in partes
diuisum pereat atque dissoluatur."

1 min. : 2 min. : 3 min. = 6° : 12° : 18°. Yet we know no relationship between 1 minute of time and an angle of 6° for they are quite incomparable.

The essence of Similitude is thus the comparing of relationships. Often for simplicity's sake only one relationship is compared, and especially often is this the case in the occidental similitudes which Jülicher takes as his norm. Fiebig, taking Jewish similitudes as his norm, regards several relationships as the usual case. He says[1] "In the method of laying stress on individual points, which belongs to the Jewish way of expressing oneself, it is specially easy to make a similitude, so to speak, with several peaks, i.e. not to give it quite strictly merely one idea, one point of comparison, as the abstract logician and refining Professor is anxious to do in his colourless theory." Jülicher had in fact defined Similitude as[2] "that figure of speech in which the working of a sentence (a thought) is made clear by laying alongside a similar sentence, whose working is known, belonging to another sphere." By restricting this definition to one sentence or one thought Jülicher ignores the possibility of several thoughts being compared. But Fiebig is quite incorrect in laying this omission to the account of a love of logic. Greater attention to logical and scientific accuracy in the definition might have avoided it. Nor is Fiebig right when he hints that the Jewish method of

[1] *op. cit.* p. 27. [2] *op. cit.*, 1 Teil, p. 80.

comparing several relationships is due to an oriental absence of logic: the number of relationships compared depends on the whim of the writer or speaker, and is not of the essence of similitude. And one more point: the purpose of a similitude may often be to force a judgment on some question, but that again is not essential.

It will be seen that both in the matter of the essential judgment brought out by a similitude, and also in the number of relationships compared in a similitude, we have departed from Jülicher's opinion, although he rightly sees the characteristic of allegory in individual traits, the two halves of the allegory being comparable element with element. We are obliged to disagree with him even more than this, for he asserts that figurative speech must be either pure allegory or pure similitude. He gets this result, as will be explained later, by his treatment of the purpose of these different forms of speech. Before dealing with the purpose, we can easily see that pure allegory and pure similitude are not the only nor even the commonest kinds of pictorial speech. The ordinary mind, and especially the mind of an Oriental, does not restrict itself within these logical bounds. The 'corruption' of pure allegory or similitude can proceed from either side. An allegory may have some of the features of similitude, or vice versa. The example that follows of an allegory which has a trace of similitude in it is rather long; a shorter specimen would have served our purpose equally well, were it not that both Jülicher and Weinel give this particular piece as a specimen of pure allegory. The original is a piece of verse by Rückert: the translation is as literal as possible.

"A man was walking in Syria leading a camel by the bridle. Suddenly with terrible mien the animal began to shy. So frightfully did it snort, that the man was obliged to run away. He ran, and saw a well there by chance on the wayside. He heard the animal breathing behind him, and that must have taken away his reasoning powers. He crept into the shaft of the well; he did not sink, but was still suspended there. A blackberry bush had grown out of the broken mouth of the well, and on to it the man held firmly, and there bewailed his fate. Looking upwards he saw the camel's head again frightfully near, which before had wanted to seize him. Then he looked down into the well and saw on the ground a dragon gaping upwards with wide open jaws, which was waiting below to gulp him down as soon as he should fall beneath. And as the poor man hung there between the two, he saw yet a third : in the crevices of the wall into which went the root of the bush on which he hung, he saw a couple of mice, quite quiet, one black the other white. He saw the black one changing with the white one in biting at the root. They gnawed, tugged, dug, burrowed and cleared the earth away from the root. And as it trickled down, the dragon below looked up to see how soon the shrub would be uprooted and fall with its burden. In anxiety, fear and trouble, surrounded, besieged and threatened on every side by reason of his pitiable suspension, he saw no hope of salvation for him. And then just as he looked round him he saw a small branch full of ripe blackberries nodding from the bush. He couldn't control his longing. He no longer saw the camel's rage, nor the dragon in the water, nor the malicious game of the mice, when the berries

struck his eye. He let the animal above go on roaring, the
dragon below him lying in wait, the mice near him gnawing : he
grasped after the berries with pleasure ; they seemed to him to
be good to eat, and he ate berry after berry joyfully, and through
their sweetness was all his fear forgotten.

Thou askest, Who is the foolish man who can in this way
forget his fear ? Then know, O Friend, thou art the man.
Listen also to the explanation. The dragon at the bottom of
the well is death's gaping throat. The camel threatening from
above is the anxiety and trouble of life. It is thou who must
hang suspended betwixt life and death on the green bush of the
world. The two mice which gnaw the roots supporting the
branches and thee, to deliver thee into the power of death, are
day and night. The black one gnaws secretly, well hidden, from
evening till morning ; the white one digging under the roots
gnaws from morning till evening. And among this stuff and
rubbish, the berry, voluptuousness, entices thee, so that thou
forgettest the camel, life's trouble, the dragon on the ground,
death, and the mice, day and night, and carest for nothing ; as
thou seizest many a berry, thou art enjoying the fruit that comes
from the well-crevices of the grave."

Taken as a whole this is a good specimen of allegory.
Apart from the first part of the story up to where the
man hung suspended, which is merely by way of
introduction, element after element in the story corresponds with element after element in the explanation.
Berry corresponds with voluptuousness because of its
sweet attraction, the black mouse corresponds to night
because of its blackness, the man corresponds with the
reader because of his thoughtlessness (a common failing
which the author would correct). Yet in one point it
fails to be pure allegory. It will be remembered that

in allegory only the elements are altered and not the relationships. Hence to get the real meaning of an allegory it is only necessary to substitute the corresponding elements mentioned in the explanation. Doing so with this allegory all goes well until just near the end, and then it fails. Thus putting in the corresponding elements it reads:

"He couldn't control his longing. He no longer saw the troubles of life, nor the fear of death, nor the malicious game of day and night, when the voluptuousness struck his eye. He let life go on troubling, death lying in wait, day and night gnawing, he grasped after the voluptuousness with pleasure; it seemed to him to be good to eat, and he ate voluptuousness after voluptuousness joyfully, and through its sweetness all his fear was forgotten."

The last few lines are absolute nonsense, because we have altered the elements and not the relationships. To make sense we must alter 'gnawing' to 'causing care and worry,' 'grasped' to 'sought after,' 'good to eat' to 'good to enjoy.' In other words this so-called allegory finishes off with similitude, for not only are new elements put into the story but new relationships. The whole weight of the story at this point rests upon the fact that the man's relationship with the berries is similar to the reader's relationship with the pleasures of life. Features of similitude have been introduced into what else had been pure allegory. It is specially instructive that those who believe that there is no half-way house between allegory and similitude should have chosen as their example of allegory one which contains these features of similitude.

Let us now consider how corruption from logical purity may proceed from the other side, and a similitude may have in it traces of allegory. Allegory enters in as soon as an element in the picture-half is compared with an element in the thought to be conveyed. In the following example from the Talmud[1], not only is the relationship of God to men compared with that of a king to his servants, but the king corresponds to God, and the servants correspond to men:

"'And the Spirit returns to God who gave it.' Give it Him in purity as He gave it thee in purity. A parable. It is like a king of flesh and blood who allotted royal garments to his servants. The wise among them folded them up and laid them in a box. The foolish among them went off and did their work in them. After certain days the king demanded his garments. The wise among them brought them back to him cleaned as they were; the foolish among them brought them back to him dirtied as they were. Then was the king pleased with the wise and angry with the foolish. Of the wise the king said, 'My garments can be put into the treasure room, and they can go to their houses in peace.' Of the foolish he said, 'My garments can be sent to the washerman, and they can be shut up in prison.'—So saith the Holy One (blessed be He) of the body of the righteous, 'He entereth into peace; they rest on their beds.' And of their soul He saith, 'And the life of my lord shall be bound in the bundle of the living.' Of the body of the wicked He saith, 'There is no peace saith Yahweh for the wicked.' And of their soul He saith, 'And the life of thine enemies shall He sling away in the hollow of a sling.'"

[1] Fiebig, *op. cit.* p. 94.

These illustrations given at the end show plainly that
the author intended the reader to think of the king as
God and of the servants as good and wicked men.   This
simple allegorising is common, and we shall see later
that it enters into many of the parables of Jesus.   The
principles here laid down of mixed allegory and similitude obtain in all sorts of cases, and not only in ancient
or oriental forms of speech.   The next example of a
similitude with traces of allegory is from Tennyson
(Ode on the death of the Duke of Wellington):

> " Not once or twice in our fair island story,
>   The path of duty was the way to glory :
>   He, that ever following her commands,
>   On with toil of heart and knees and hands,
>   Thro' the long gorge to the far light has won
>   His path upward, and prevail'd,
>   Shall find the toppling crags of Duty scaled
>   Are close upon the shining table-lands
>   To which our God Himself is moon and sun."

The main part of this is similitude, comparing the
difficulties of following duty, and the glory to follow,
with the toil and labour of climbing up a gorge on to
the table-land above and the glorious sunshine found
there.   (Note, by the way, that several relationships
are compared and not one only.)   But then the last
line, in which God is compared with the moon and
sun as the source of light, is a mark of allegory.   One
more example may be given, this time from Latin

classics, to prove the universality of this mixed form of speech[1]:

"Nam ut tempestates saepe certo aliquo coeli signo commouentur, saepe improuisae nulla ex certa ratione obscura aliqua ex causa concitantur : sic in hac comitiorum tempestate populari saepe intelligas, quo signo commota sit, saepe ita obscura est, ut sine causa excitata uideatur."

Lagrange[2] in commenting on this passage says "Strict parable would confine itself to comparing what happens in a tempest with what happens in the comitia. When Cicero calls the popular agitation a tempest he mixes a little allegory with the parable. So far is it true that the two species are rarely found in an absolutely pure state, because one more willingly compares two situations when the principal object of the one has something analogous with the principal object of the other."

This demonstration of the existence of forms of speech having the properties both of allegory and of similitude will set us at much greater ease when we come to deal with the parables of Jesus. For neither the attempt to make them into nothing but allegory, nor the attempt to make them nothing but similitude, appeals to us as a fair and reasonable treatment of the words.

[1] Cicero, *Pro Murena*, 17.
[2] *Revue Biblique Internationale* 1909, " La parabole en dehors de l'Évangile," par Fr. M.-J. Lagrange, p. 212.

CHAPTER II

THE PURPOSE OF FIGURATIVE SPEECH

Any departure from the straightforward, bald, literal method of expressing oneself needs an explanation. What is the reason and purpose, that not only in poetry and prose but in our daily conversation we continually bring in conceptions from a sphere other than that under discussion? Such figurative expressions as 'setting the Thames on fire' or 'beating about the bush' are always on our lips. Nor is the tendency confined to the educated classes. Those whose conversation is so simple that they prefer to use the present tense and oratio recta ('he says to me') use figurative speech no less than those who might be suspected of a desire to embellish their sentences. With what object are simile and metaphor so commonly used, and is it the same object that encourages the use of the more complicated forms of similitude and allegory?

There is no doubt that simile and similitude are used in order to help the hearer or reader to understand. Especially when dealing with abstract subjects which treat of things only partially understood, it is found in practice that the thought can be made clearer by comparison with conceptions, belonging to another sphere, whose relationships are well known. It is in accordance with this tendency that primitive races personified various forces of nature. The only self-acting forces of which they knew were those of living beings, and hence they thought of the natural forces of storm or of vitality as the workings of gods and goddesses. The use of idols also was a method of expressing in similitude some of the characteristics of the god, who could not be directly perceived by the senses. The idol did not, it is true, express all the characteristics of the god, and it was for that reason that their use in the worship of Yahweh was objected to by the Jewish prophets. The same is true of all similes and similitudes: they do express part of the relationship correctly, but only a part. But for the sake of instruction it is a step forward to teach a part, and therefore simile and similitude are useful methods of imparting truths. Their limitations are easily seen. The soul may be said to long after God as a hart desires the water-brooks; but the desire of the hart is animal and primitive, compared with the spiritual and deep longing of the soul for God. So it is also in every similitude. In the one quoted above, p. 6, of Rabbi Akiba, the relationships existing between the Jews and their Law and the foreign power are explained and

made clearer by means of the figurative story. Yet
that story only expresses the truth imperfectly. Such
an imperfect explanation is better than nothing. The
need for it lies in the poverty of language; for even
though the thought might have been expressed better
in straightforward speech if cast into philosophic form,
the hearers' knowledge of the language would not be
sufficient to enable them to understand. In other
words in speaking of the limitations of language we
must remember the hearers as well as the speaker.
It is because of these limitations that similitude, in
appealing from the unknown to the known, becomes
a common and natural way of making clear what would
otherwise be difficult to comprehend.

The purpose of allegory is in some respects different
from that of similitude. To put it in a few words: the
purpose of similitude is to explain higher conceptions
by means of lower ones, but the purpose of allegory is
to draw the thoughts from one set of conceptions to
another, generally of course from a lower to a higher
plane. When an allegory is told it is at first sight
a riddle. It tells only of earthly things, but the
hearer's interest is gained when he is told that something higher lies hidden behind. As soon as the steps
are given by which the earthly story discloses its
heavenly meaning, the hearer instinctively mounts by
those steps to the higher conceptions. Those conceptions
are not made any easier to understand by this method,

but the attention of the hearer is caught to them.
That this is the purpose with which allegory is introduced
may be seen in the example given above—the allegory
of Jotham. Neither the characters of the men concerned,
nor their relationships with one another, are expressed
any more clearly or simply than they could have been in
straightforward speech. But had Jotham begun to set
forth his case in plain words he would have had no
hearers; the form in which he threw his speech attracted
attention, because until the end of his remarks it was
not clear exactly to what he was referring. It appears
from this that to construct an allegory needs a certain
art or skill, although when told it can be understood by
the simplest minds. For this reason we find that the
figurative speech of uneducated people is mostly of the
form of similitude or of simple metaphor, but not
allegory; but if those same people are told an allegory
they will understand and enjoy it.

This leads us to a feature of figurative speech which
is important in Jülicher's train of reasoning. A pictorial
form of speech is incomplete until it is clearly set forth
wherein the comparison lies. This is true both in
allegory and in similitude. E.g. it implies nothing
spiritual simply to say "The hart desireth the water-
brooks," but it needs the explanatory addition "So
longeth my soul after Thee, O God." So also with
allegory, Jotham's fable would teach nothing unless it
were made clear that the bramble was Abimelech, and so

on. Here Jülicher makes a strange assumption, that while allegory needs an explanation, similitude needs none. The reason which led him to this is probably in part that the explanation of a similitude is given as a rule in the story itself, while that of an allegory is generally given afterwards; partly also because the explanation of an allegory has to deal with each individual trait, and is therefore fuller than that of a similitude in which only the few relationships which are compared have to be mentioned. That similitudes need explanation can easily be seen by observing that no instruction is given by the mere statement, " A man took a grain of mustard seed and sowed it in his field, etc." In order to convey teaching it is necessary to add that the kingdom of Heaven is like it. Again there are cases where the explanation of a similitude comes at the end; this is specially the case when several relationships are to be compared, e.g. Rabbi Akiba's similitude given above concludes with the following explanation: " So we too: if we fear now where we sit and busy ourselves with the Law, in which it stands written, 'For that is thy life and the length of thy days,' how much more if we go off and are neglectful of it?" This explanation makes clear which are the relationships in the story compared with those in the experiences of the Jews of that time.

Attention must further be paid to the form in which the explanation is given. In accordance with the different nature of allegory and similitude the explanation is differently expressed. For allegory it should logically take the form of "*a* stands for *A* (by reason of some similarity)." Actually it is generally "*a* is *A* "; so e.g. "the black mouse is night (because it is dark), the white mouse is day (because it is light)." The form in which the explanation is given of Jotham's allegory is on the face of it different ("Now therefore, if ye have dealt truly and sincerely, in that ye have made Abimelech king..."); but it says implicitly "the bramble is Abimelech," because in the story the bramble had been made king.

The form of explanation required for a similitude should be logically, "The relationships existing in this sphere are similar to the relationships in that sphere." It is in this form in the parable of the fig tree: "Behold the fig tree and all the trees: when they now shoot forth ye see and know of your own selves that the summer is now nigh. Even so ye also, when ye see these things coming to pass, know ye that the kingdom of God is nigh." Such a method of expression is however not often favoured, but the explanation is introduced by what looks like an allegorical comparison: "The kingdom of Heaven is like unto a man that is a merchant seeking goodly pearls." There is really no similarity between the kingdom of Heaven and a merchant, nor is it intended; the inconsistency is merely one of expression, and Jülicher is quite right in saying[1] that the intended meaning is " In the kingdom of Heaven the condition of affairs is as in this story." Fiebig seems to have missed this point, for while observing the inconsistency as it stands[2], he thinks that it is corrected by understanding " The kingdom of Heaven is like a very costly pearl." In reality that is equally inconsistent, because the kingdom of Heaven is not compared with a pearl, but the seeking for the kingdom is compared with the seeking for a pearl. An instructive case for the explanation of a similitude is that of the unmerciful servant, for there there is a double explanation, the first one inconsistent at the beginning of the parable " The kingdom of Heaven is likened unto a certain king," and the second logically correct at the end of the parable " So shall also my heavenly Father do unto you if ye forgive not everyone his brother from your hearts." The inconsistency of the former method of explanation is of no importance so long as we know about it, because it is then easily understood. At times, as for instance in the parable of the wicked husbandmen, the explanation is not given at all in so many words but lies in the context from which it can easily be gathered. Lagrange says[3] " Il importe très peu que la lumière vienne d'une particule comparative explicite ou de la situation elle-même."

We are now in a position to enquire what purpose

[1] *op. cit.* 1 Teil, p. 98.   [2] *op. cit.* p. 13.
[3] *Revue Biblique Internationale* 1909, p. 205.

underlies the use of mixed similitudes and allegories such as we have described. The departure from the pure forms is a natural and easy process. Take first the allegory with a trace of similitude in it. It has been pointed out that skill is required to construct a good allegory, and that when it is made it only serves the purpose of directing the attention to some higher sphere. Presumably the writer has it at heart to give instruction about this higher sphere, and therefore it is both natural and easy for him to do as Rückert has done in his allegory, and introduce a trace of similitude. This trace of similitude gives some instruction about the higher sphere to which the mind has been directed by means of the allegory. On the other hand the traces of allegory which enter into similitude are half accidental[1] and half serve to explain the thing to be told. This may seem strange to those who have fallen into the trap of regarding allegory as serving only to make blind and dull and to stupefy. When our Lord said "How often would I have gathered thy children together even as a hen gathereth her chickens under her wings" He spoke pure simile, for in no way could He be compared with a hen; but when He uses the similitude of king and subjects to express the relationship between God and men we feel at once that He is thinking of God as king, i.e. in terms of allegory. The same we found in the Jewish parable quoted on p. 14;

[1] See Lagrange's remark quoted on p. 16.

and in the quotation from Tennyson we found God allegorically compared with sun and moon as source of light. These traces of allegory have not obscured the meaning. And for the ordinary mind, which does not distinguish between the comparison of relationships and the comparison of elements, it is quite fitting that if God be related to men as a king to his subjects, God should be also comparable in some way to a king.

There is one point of which Jülicher makes much that must be mentioned. He divides figurative speech into *eigentlich* and *uneigentlich*. *Eigentlich* speech is straightforward, or true, saying what is meant, while in *uneigentlich* one thing is said and another thing meant. We might translate them 'proper' and 'improper' in the same sort of sense that those words are used of arithmetical fractions. He regards similitudes as proper and allegories as improper speech. This distinction depends on his statement, with which we do not agree, that allegories need an explanation but that similitudes do not. In either case the speech must rather be regarded as improper if, or so long as, no explanation is given, and then, when explained, it may be regarded as proper.

CHAPTER III

THE NATURE OF THE PARABLES OF THE SYNOPTIC GOSPELS

The word used in the Synoptic Gospels to describe the parables is παραβολή. If this name is to help in the explanation of the parables, we must enquire what meaning it had among Jewish writers. The Synoptists were greatly influenced by the O.T. and especially by the LXX translation of it. The word παραβολή is fairly common in the LXX, and almost always as representing the word מָשָׁל (*mashal*).

Jülicher has already shown that the only meaning which can be traced in common between the varied uses of the word *mashal* is that of figurative speech. But it will perhaps be profitable to enquire further how the different meanings of the word are linked together.

Starting with the general connotation of something figurative, we have first those short sayings handed from mouth to mouth which are called proverbs. Many of these have nothing figurative in them, e.g. Ezek. xii.

22, 23 " What is this proverb that ye have in the land
of Israel, saying, The days are prolonged and every
vision faileth ?...but say unto them, The days are at
hand and every vision is (?) established," or 1 Sam. xxiv.
13 " As saith the proverb of the ancients, Out of the
wicked cometh forth wickedness."   The name of *mashal*
was no doubt attached to these because others of the
same sort are figurative, e.g. Ezek. xviii. 2 " The fathers
have eaten sour grapes and the children's teeth are set
on edge," and probably also 1 Sam. x. 12 " It became a
proverb, Is Saul also among the prophets ? "   In just
the same way in English we include in the one category
of proverbs a straightforward saying like " Where there's
a will there's a way " and a figurative expression like
" A cat may look at a king."   From the meaning of
proverb the word *mashal* passes easily into the sense of
a by-word.   For if a proverb arises about a person, a
nation or a city, it can easily become a cutting remark,
and the person of whom it is said becomes a by-word.
In this sense *mashal* is often used as a threat of what
may happen to Israel, e.g. Deut. xxviii. 37, 1 Kings ix. 7,
Jer. xxiv. 9, 2 Chron. vii. 20, Ezek. xiv. 8, and in the
first four of these cases the word is paralleled by שְׁנִינָה
' a cutting remark.'

Starting again from the original sense of figurative
speech, we find *mashal* used for such speech as the
poems of Balaam (Num. xxiii. and xxiv.) which contain
some elements of metaphor or simile.   From this use

others are developed in which it is harder to find traces of anything figurative. First, odes such as Num. xxi. 27–30, about Heshbon, and short sentences of ethical wisdom like those of which Solomon is said to have spoken 3000, and those contained in the Book of Proverbs. Of the latter it has been pointed out that x. 1–xxii. 16 and xxv.–xxix. are called *meshalim* in the stricter sense (see x. 1 and xxv. 1), but that i. 1 describes the whole contents of the book as *meshalim*. Secondly, any discourse which is high-flown like Balaam's, though it may lack any figurative element, may be described as *mashal*. Examples are Isai. xiv. 4 "Thou shalt take up this parable against the king of Babylon, and say, How hath the oppressor ceased, the boisterous behaviour ceased," Mic. ii. 4 "They shall take up a parable against you, and lament with a doleful lamentation, and say, We be utterly spoiled...," Hab. ii. 6 "Shall not all these take up a parable against him, and a taunting riddle (חִידָה) against him, saying, Woe to him that increaseth that which is not his!" From this sense is developed the idea of the speech of the wise and learned. So Prov. xxvi. 7 "The legs of the lame hang loose; so is a parable in the mouth of fools," and Eccles. xii. 9 "Because the Preacher was wise, he still taught the people knowledge; yea he pondered and sought out and set in order many parables." And since the learned often say things which the unwise and unlearned fail to understand, the word *mashal* in this use is often compared with חִידָה 'dark saying' or 'riddle':

Ps. xlix. 3   "My mouth shall speak wisdom;
      And the meditation of my heart shall be of understanding.
      I will incline my ear to a parable:
      I will open my dark saying upon the harp."

Ps. lxxviii. 2 "I will open my mouth in a parable:
      I will utter dark sayings of old."

It will be observed that at least in these two passages the poet does not propose to propound a dark saying but to declare one. He intended to expound something which had been hidden from venerable antiquity. The parable was his method of explaining the ancient mystery. Mention must here be made of Prov. i. 6 where four expressions are laid alongside: מָשָׁל וּמְלִיצָה דִּבְרֵי חֲכָמִים וְחִידֹתָם "a parable and an enigma, words of the wise and their dark sayings." Here *mashal* is specially co-ordinated with 'words of the wise' which is its nearest synonym in the sense in which it is used in this book; and מליצה is specially co-ordinated with חידה, the meaning of the first being either 'satire' or perhaps more probably 'enigma,' and the meaning of the second 'dark sayings,' both probably rather in the sense of difficult moral problems than of riddles made intentionally difficult. In these examples all thought of figurative speech seems to have gone, or to be in the

background, but in Ezekiel we find it again in the
form of allegory: Ezek. xvii. 2 "Son of man, put forth
a riddle and speak a parable unto the house of Israel"
followed by the allegory of the vine and the two eagles;
Ezek. xxiv. 3 "Utter a parable unto the rebellious
house" followed by the allegory of the cauldron. The
original meaning of something figurative, which had all
but disappeared owing to the secondary associations of
the word *mashal*, has returned. In Ezek. xvii. 2 it is
paralleled more or less with 'riddle' or 'dark saying,'
and, what we shall find of especial interest, in the eyes
of some of the people a parable meant something
difficult to understand, for the prophet complains (xx. 49)
"Ah, Lord God! they say of me, Is he not a speaker of
parables?"

In the Apocrypha the word παραβολή bears meanings similar to those which it had in the O.T. proper as
the translation of *mashal*. In Tob. iii. 4 and Wisd. v.
3 there occurs the expression παραβολὴ ὀνειδισμοῦ
meaning a by-word. The sense of a difficult problem
is given to the word *similitudo* in 4 Esdras iv. 3
"et respondit mihi et dixit: tres uias missus sum
ostendere tibi, et tres similitudines proponere coram te;
de quibus si mihi renunciaueris unam ex his, et ego
tibi demonstrabo uiam quam desideras uidere, et doceam
te quare cor malignum. Et dixi: loquere dominus
meus. et dixit ad me: uade, pondera mihi ignis
pondus, aut mensura mihi satum uenti, aut reuoca mihi

diem quae praeteriit." The word is also used for what is a pure similitude, viii. 2 "Dicam autem coram te similitudinem, Ezra, quomodo autem interrogas terram et dicet tibi quoniam dabit terram multam magis unde fiat fictile, paruum autem puluerem unde aurum fit, sic et actus praesentis saeculi: Multi quidem creati sunt pauci autem saluabuntur[1]." In Enoch chaps. xxxvii.–lxxi. the Ethiopian word *mesale* refers to apocalyptic visions. They are probably so called as being mysterious things in course of being revealed, cf. e.g. Enoch lxviii. 1 "And after that my grandfather Enoch gave the signs of all the secréts in a book, and the similitudes which had been given to him, and he put them together for me in the words of the book of the Similitudes." In B. Sir. xx. 27 the heading λόγοι παραβολῶν (which is probably genuine, though omitted by some cursives and the Syro-hexaplar) is followed not by anything figurative but by words of ethical wisdom. But it is in the sense of the speech of the wise that παραβολή chiefly occurs in B. Sir., and the passages are deserving of close study[2]. In xxxviii. 33 we are told that artificers shall not be found where parables are, ἐν παραβολαῖς οὐχ εὑρεθήσονται, because their minds are too fully occupied with their manual labour. It is among those who do not think, that parables are so out

---

[1] Ed. Bensly and James, *Texts and Studies*, iii. 2.

[2] In dealing with B. Sir. I am indebted to the edition by J. H. A. Hart.

of place, xx. 20 " A parable from a fool's mouth will be
rejected, for he will not speak it in its season." The
same is found in the reading of אᶜᵃ in xxi. 16 " A fool's
discourse is as a burden in the way, but a parable shall
be found on the lips of the understanding." Like all
godly things parables are profitable for the wise, but an
abomination to the sinner, i. 25 ἐν θησαυροῖς σοφίας
παραβολαὶ ἐπιστήμης, βδέλυγμα δὲ ἁμαρτωλῷ θεο-
σέβεια. Those who think and pay attention can
understand parables, iii. 29 " The heart of the prudent
will understand a parable, and the ear of a listener is
the desire of a wise man." A most important instance
is xiii. 26 where the Hebrew has " Withdrawing and
study, toilsome thoughts" but the Greek εὕρησις
παραβολῶν διαλογισμοὶ μετὰ κόπου. The Greek
εὕρησις is a mistranslation of the word שׂיִג (' withdrawing ') taking it as from the √גִשׂיַ instead of from
√סוּג or שׂוּג; and παραβολῶν is given as the chief
example of musing or contemplative study. At the
same time the translator must have considered that
the interpretation of parables was a toilsome business,
although the expression of the idea here came quite
accidentally as we have seen. Two more passages help
us to discover wherein the difficulty of parables lies.
xxxix. 2, 3 "He that hath applied his soul, and meditateth
on the Law of the Most High...shall enter into the
intricacies of parables (ἐν στροφαῖς παραβολῶν)...and
be conversant in the obscurities of parables (ἐν αἰνίγμασι

παραβολῶν)." αἴνιγμα does not necessarily mean a riddle made artificially difficult, but may be something intrinsically difficult as in 1 Cor. xiii. 12 " Now we see through a mirror ἐν αἰνίγματι." The text of Ben Sira before us shows that the difficulties of parables do not need art or skill to overcome but only devoutness. A parable then according to this writer is not thought of as something made artificially difficult like a riddle[1]. The obscurity and intricacy lie in the subject with which the parable deals. The other passage is B. Sir. xlvii. 15, 17 " Thy soul covered the earth and thou filledst it with parables of riddles (παραβολαῖς αἰνιγμάτων)....In songs and proverbs and parables and in interpretations (ἐν ᾠδαῖς καὶ παροιμίαις καὶ παραβολαῖς καὶ (ἐν) ἑρμηνείαις) countries marvelled at thee." The Hebrew in verse 17 begins בשיר משל חידה ומליצה recalling the passage in Prov. i. 6 quoted above. In that passage מליצה and חידה are co-ordinated. Here מליצה is translated ἑρμηνεία 'interpretation' instead of its other possible meaning of 'enigma.' Hence it is probable that the translator thought of חידה as

[1] Lagrange is probably more or less correct in asserting the same of Hebrew use generally (*Revue Biblique Internationale*, 1909, p. 350): " Si diverses que soient ses manifestations (i.e. of parables) elles ont le plus souvent quelque chose d'artificiel, de recherché et de figuré, mais on n'y trouverait jamais l'intention de cacher une verité, ni même aucune tentative de s'adresser à un groupe choisi d'auditeurs qui comprendront le sens ésotérique, dissimulé au grand public."

'a difficult problem' and not in its alternative possible meaning of 'enigma.' Jülicher is therefore not justified in saying that παραβολή means a riddle because it here represents חירה[1]. The translator probably thought of חידה as 'a difficult problem' and accordingly translated it by παραβολή.

The main conclusion which we draw from this survey of the use of παραβολή by Ben Sira is that, though the word preserved some of the variety of meaning which it had in the translation of the O.T., the author tends to use it in the more restricted sense of the speech of the wise.

In later Judaism a special kind of speech was known as parable. Its object was to impart instruction; it was always figurative. It was introduced simply by the word מָשָׁל, or by מָשְׁלוּ מָשָׁל "they tell a parable"; or by אֶמְשׁוֹל לְךָ מָשָׁל "I will tell thee a parable." Examples of these Jewish parables have already been given. Fiebig in his book *Die Gleichnisreden Jesu*, 1912, collects a number of these parables originating in the first and early second centuries, from the school of Hillel and Shammai to R. Akiba. As we have already seen from the examples given these

---

[1] *op. cit.* 1 Teil, p. 39 : "um so interessanter für uns ist die Thatsache, dass der übersetzende Siracide חידה (Rätsel) mit παραβολή wiedergiebt : dem entspricht der übrige Gebrauch des Wortes in dem griechischen Buche."

parables embrace similitude in which more than one relationship is compared, and also in some cases they embrace allegory. We find that the word 'parable' has acquired a restricted meaning, leaving out the old connotations of 'by-word,' 'proverb,' 'sentence of ethical wisdom' and so forth, just as Ben Sira had practically restricted the use of the word to the sense of the language of the wise. These Jewish parables are nearest in time and origin to the parables of our Lord, so that in dealing with the latter we shall find no greater help from outside than the contemporary Jewish parables. It is significant that Jülicher altogether ignores them. But when Weinel, after reading some of Fiebig's work, says[1], "Für die Methode der Gleichniserzählung haben wir also gar nichts aus dem Talmud zu lernen," we may take it that he is chiefly prompted to do so by the bitterness of his attack on Fiebig. On the other hand we cannot judge Jesus' parables merely from those of His contemporaries. In so many points He broke away from the ways and traditions of the Jewish teachers of His time that we must be prepared for originality here also. Like every great genius He was not altogether moulded by history, but rather forced history to conform itself to Him, a fact which Albert Schweitzer brings out forcibly. We who believe in the Resurrection need not go further with that scholar when he thinks that

[1] *Z. nt. W.* 1912, Heft 2, "Der Talmud, die Gleichniss Jesu und die synoptische Frage," p. 120.

Jesus' design to mould history ended in being Himself crushed by it.

With this preparation we turn to the Synoptic Gospels themselves to judge the nature of the speeches which are described as parables. The word παραβολή does not occur in the Fourth Gospel, and the figurative speech put into our Lord's mouth in that Gospel needs a separate treatment (Chapter V).

It is of course generally recognised that other speeches are to be regarded as parables than those few explicitly so called. For the moment however we will restrict ourselves to the passages in which the word παραβολή actually comes. In one place it is used of a proverb "Physician, heal thyself," Lc. iv. 23, though we may notice that it is spoken figuratively. Our Lord's sentence of ethical wisdom, Lc. xiv. 8 "When thou art bidden of any man to a wedding, recline not in the chief place," is called a parable, perhaps with reference to the similar remark in Prov. xxv. 6, 7, the contents of that chapter having been described as מְשָׁלִים[1]. In this example there is nothing figurative; it is merely a straightforward sentence, describing from one instance what should be men's behaviour generally towards one another. Of the remaining pieces in the Synoptic Gospels that are named parables a few are short terse statements or questions, introduced for the purpose of

---

[1] Prov. xxv. 1, but in the Greek παιδεῖαι or παροιμίαι.

comparison: Lc. vi. 39 "Can a blind man lead a blind man? will they not both fall into the ditch?" Lc. v. 36 "No man tearing a patch from a new garment putteth it on to an old garment, etc.," Mc. vii. 15 (|| Mt. xv. 11) "There is nothing from without a man entering into him that can defile him, etc.," Mc. iii. 23 "How can Satan cast out Satan? and if a kingdom be divided against itself that kingdom cannot stand, etc." In other (and more numerous) cases the comparison is carried further, producing a narrative. The stories of the Sower, the Grain of Mustard Seed, the Wicked Husbandmen, the Leaven, the Tares, the Marriage Supper, the Fig Tree, the Rich Fool, the Lost Sheep, the Unrighteous Judge, the Pharisee and the Publican, and the Pounds, are all definitely described as parables. There are many other narratives in all respects similar to these twelve which must therefore be included in the same category. It is of these narratives that we usually think when parables are mentioned.

It will be well now to consider all the different kinds of figurative speech as they appear in the Gospels, remembering that the name parable is used chiefly, but not exclusively, to describe the longer pieces which are cast into narrative form. First we notice that our Lord uses the simple forms of simile and metaphor. An example has just been referred to where He uses the two similes of a kingdom divided against itself, and a house divided against itself (Mc. iii. 23-26), to show

the absurdity of Satan being divided against himself.
Three distinct similes come in a single sentence in
Mt. x. 16 "Behold, I send you forth as sheep in the
midst of wolves; be ye therefore wise as serpents and
harmless as doves." Metaphor also is fairly frequent:
Mt. xi. 29 "Take my yoke upon you," Mt. xxiii. 16 "Woe
unto you, blind guides!" Mc. x. 38 "Are ye able to
drink the cup that I drink?" Mc. viii. 15 "Take heed,
beware of the leaven of the Pharisees and the leaven of
Herod." In the more expanded forms of speech similitude fills the largest place, while allegory is comparatively
rare. Allegory is not however altogether absent as
some have imagined: two examples may be given.
Lc. xiii. 24–29—

"Strive to enter in by the narrow door: for many, I say
unto you, shall seek to enter in, and shall not be able. When
once the master of the house is risen up, and hath shut to the door,
and ye begin to stand without, and to knock at the door, saying,
Lord, open to us; and he shall answer and say to you, I know
you not whence ye are; then shall ye begin to say, We did eat
and drink in thy presence, and thou didst teach in our streets;
and he shall say, I tell you, I know not whence ye are; depart
from me, all ye workers of iniquity. There shall be the weeping
and gnashing of teeth, when ye shall see Abraham and Isaac and
Jacob, and all the prophets, in the kingdom of God, and yourselves
cast forth without. And they shall come from the east and
west, and from the north and south, and shall sit down in the
kingdom of God."

Starting with the metaphor of the narrow door, our
Lord expands it by what follows into an allegory. The

necessary explanation is given as the allegory proceeds so that the hearers are left in no doubt that the door means the entrance into the kingdom of God, and that the Lord in whose presence they had eaten and who had taught in their streets is Jesus Christ. The other example of allegory is Lc. xi. 24–26—

" The unclean spirit when he is gone out of the man, passeth through waterless places, seeking rest; and finding none, he saith, I will turn back unto my house whence I came out. And when he is come, he findeth it swept and garnished. Then goeth he, and taketh to him seven other spirits more evil than himself; and they enter in and dwell there: and the last state of that man becometh worse than the first."

The explanation is given that the 'house' of the unclean spirit is the man whom he had possessed; waterless places where the spirit found no rest would naturally be interpreted as such conditions under which an evil spirit would not care to live; while the house swept and garnished is clearly shown by the context to mean the man himself ready to receive the evil spirit back again.

Of the similitudes used by our Lord a certain number may be classed together as example-stories (*Beispielerzählungen*). A particular case is given from which a general inference may be drawn. They differ in one respect from similitude proper. In a similitude proper, conditions obtaining in one sphere are explained by comparison with conditions obtaining in another sphere; but in an example-story the comparison is made with conditions in the same sphere. They may be called similitudes in the same sense that a circle may be called an ellipse—an ellipse in which the two foci coincide. An example that perhaps should only be put on the border of this class is Mt. xii. 11, in which our Lord appeals from the fact that His hearers would save a beast on the Sabbath, that therefore a priori it is lawful to save a human life on that day. In Lc. x. 30, Jesus answers the lawyer who asks for a definition of a neighbour by giving the story of the Good Samaritan, in which a true neighbourly action is described, that is He gives one example of the sort of behaviour that should be copied: "Go, and do thou likewise." The Rich Fool in Lc. xii. 16 who lived a thoughtless, careless life, trusting in his riches, is an example to be avoided: "so is he that layeth up treasure for himself, and is not rich towards God." The lesson that men should be humble is taught in Lc. xviii. 9 by the parable of the Pharisee and the Publican: "for every one that exalteth himself shall be humbled, and he that humbleth himself shall be exalted." The last two stories are definitely spoken of as παραβολαί. When we compare the sentence already quoted, Lc. xiv. 8, about not choosing the foremost seats, we see the connexion between these example-stories and the sentences of ethical wisdom which were called parables in the Old Testament.

In many similitudes there is only one point of

comparison. If the similitude is short that is what one would naturally expect, e.g. Mt. ix. 12, 13 "They that are whole have no need of a physician, but those that are sick...for I came not to call righteous but sinners." But it is also often the case in longer similitudes where interpreters have from time to time been tempted to find other points of comparison, e.g. in the story of the Unjust Steward, Lc. xvi. 1–8. The one point of the parable is to show that the children of this age are often wiser than the children of light. Verse 9 is really independent of the parable and we shall speak of that later[1]. Similitudes of this kind are often used argumentatively to prove some judgment. This is seen well in the story of the two Debtors, Lc. vii. 41–47. The comparison in the story is between the behaviour of debtors to their lender and the behaviour of sinners toward God. The judgment in verse 47 is that the woman's great love is a proof that her sins had been forgiven.

Besides these there are similitudes in which several relationships are compared. Such is the story of the Faithful and Wise Steward in Lc. xii. 42–48. There the faithful steward is compared with a faithful disciple of Christ, an unfaithful steward is compared with an unfaithful disciple, and the punishment of steward and disciple is compared. In these cases of several relationships there can still be one judgment arising out of the parable, as is better seen in the parable

[1] p. 86.

of the Ten Virgins, Mt. xxv. 1–13. The sudden
coming of the bridegroom is like the sudden coming of
the kingdom. The behaviour of the wise and foolish
virgins is like the watchfulness of the true disciple and
the carelessness of others. Yet the story all culminates
in one judgment, verse 13, "Watch therefore, for ye
know not the day nor the hour." But as we have
already pointed out the judgment is not an essential
part of a similitude. In a descriptive parable such as
that of the Drag-net, Mt. xiii. 47, as opposed to the
argumentative parables we have been considering, we
see a picture of the good and bad in the kingdom, and
their final separation, without any one judgment or
decision being drawn from it. The parable of the
Wicked Husbandmen, Mc. xii. 1–12, raises the interesting
question as to the number of relationships compared.
The reason for doubt is that the explanation of this
similitude is left to be given by the context. Verse 12
says that the elders perceived that He spake the
parable against them: in other words the behaviour of
the husbandmen is compared with the behaviour of
Jewish rulers. The hearers would infer that they were
to be rejected for their misbehaviour, but it remains,
and must remain, a moot point whether the parable
teaches, as the reason for their rejection, that they had
rejected the prophets and the Messiah. We must
remember in this and in other cases that at best we
have only partially the context. Points like those

mentioned, which we may guess at, would probably be quite clear to the original hearers from what had been said ten minutes before.

In two cases S. Luke gives us a combination of a metaphor with two similitudes. The first, xii. 35–40, is spoken of as a whole as παραβολή. It begins with the metaphor "Let your loins be girded about and your lamps burning," then goes on, verse 36, with a similitude comparing the disciples with men awaiting their lord after his wedding. Then in verse 39 is another similitude in which the disciples' watchfulness is compared with that of a householder watching for a thief. The whole 'parable' is summed up by verse 40 "Be ye also ready: for in an hour that ye think not, the Son of Man cometh." The second case of this sort of combination is Lc. xiv. 27–33. First there is the metaphor "Whosoever doth not take up his cross and come after me cannot be my disciple," then the similitudes (verse 28) about the man building a tower, and (verse 31) about a king going to war. The whole passage is cemented together by the concluding verse 33 "So therefore whosoever he be of you that renounceth not all that he hath, he cannot be my disciple."

The interpretation of the parable of the Rich Man and Lazarus, Lc. xvi. 19–31, is one of no ordinary difficulty. There are practically three ways in which it has been treated, (1) to lay all the stress on the first part up to verse 26 and see an example-story of how the luxurious go to Hell and the down-trodden to Heaven; (2) to lay all the stress on the latter part in which the abiding value of the Old Testament is taught; and (3) to suppose that the parable is really a conflate production, so that both parts would have to be interpreted separately according to their original context. Of these three possibilities we can say this: if we can get help from the present context in S. Luke we must use it, because if the parable does not now stand in its original context we have no means at all of deciding between the three alternatives. Arguing then from the present context: in verse 14 we read that the Pharisees were money-lovers, in verse 15 that although they justified themselves before men God's judgment was different. Verses 16, 17 say that the Law existed up till John the Baptist, and that although all sorts of people try to force their way into the kingdom of God they will fail unless they still obey the Law, because God's Law is eternal. Verse 18 is an example of how people have tried in vain to break one of God's laws with impunity. Then comes the parable. And at the conclusion it reads "If they hear not Moses and the prophets, neither will they be persuaded if one rise from the dead." With such a context the parable must surely teach the abiding value of the Law. This does not however exclude interpretation of the first part of the parable. We may describe it as a similitude which for the larger part has become an example-story. The first part of it reminds the hearers that the Law which they have always believed in—which teaches reward for the good, the poor, and the afflicted, and punishment for the wicked and oppressors—will still hold. The second part teaches that the Law will continue to remain a greater evidence of God than any such miracle as a message from the unseen world. The stress naturally lies on this second part, because the subject of the first part, the reward and punishment in the next world, was already known to all the hearers.

The parable of the Prodigal Son, Lc. xv. 11—32, has suffered enough, but not quite such opposing interpretations as Dives and Lazarus. Again we must turn to the context, and the context in this case consists of the preceding parables of the Lost Sheep and the Lost Drachma. Those two are pure similitudes, which are carefully explained, in verses 7 and 10 respectively, of the joy in heaven over the repentance of one sinner. In neither of these similitudes are there any traces of allegory: there is no resemblance between either a sheep or a drachma and a human soul—in spite of the ancient attempt to see in the king's image on the coin a resemblance to the soul made in the image of God! But in the case of the Prodigal Son the son *is* a human soul. The spheres of the story and of the thought to be compared are not just the same, so as to make an example-story like Dives and Lazarus, but the sameness of several of the chief features, the soul, the sin, the

conversion, the father, and the home, in the story and in
the thought to be conveyed, gives us traits of allegory.
It is in fact that accidental admixture of allegory which
is referred to in the quotation from Lagrange on page
16 above.

Small allegorical traits are fairly frequent. The
parable of the Unmerciful Servant, Mt. xviii. 21–35, is
on the whole a good similitude, the relationships between
slaves and one another and their king being compared
with those between men and their fellows and God.
But we find here, just as in many Talmudic parables,
the king allegorically representing God, and the slaves
representing men as the servants of God. Another
connexion with the Rabbinic parables is the expression
used here ἀνθρώπῳ βασιλεῖ which corresponds to the
expression "a king of flesh and blood." An allegorical
trait of some interest comes in the parable of the Grain
of Mustard Seed, Mc. iv. 30–32. After describing the
growth of the seed from minuteness to very great size,
as comparable with the growth of the kingdom of God,
it continues "so that under its shadow the birds of the
heaven can lodge." Taken alone we might merely
regard this as a picturesque addition, but the phrase
was already a familiar one as representing the safety of
the weak under the protection of the strong. As such
we find in Judg. ix. 15 "put your trust in my shadow,"
in Ezek. xxxi. 6 "all the fowls of heaven made their
nests in his boughs...and under his shadow dwelt

all great nations," and in the allegorical interpretation of Nebuchadnezzar's dream, Dan. iv. 20–22 "the tree... under which the beasts of the field dwelt, and upon whose branches the fowls of the heaven had their habitation: it is thou, O king, that art grown and become strong: for thy greatness is grown and reacheth unto heaven, and thy dominion to the end of the earth." We are therefore bound by the previous use of this phrase to interpret allegorically that people will find safety under the rule and protection of the kingdom of God.

The two parables of the Sower and the Tares need a special treatment, because the explanations with which they are provided have brought them specially into the fire of criticism. They are dealt with in the next chapter.

Looking back on the figurative speech of our Lord as we have glanced at it in this chapter, we see no such uniformity as has been imagined by those who wished to regard everything as similitude. In fact almost every kind of figurative speech is represented more or less, although it is of course true that similitude fills the larger part. To a considerable variety the name παραβολή is expressly given, forming a link with various forms of speech used in the Old Testament and Apocrypha which bear the name מָשָׁל or παραβολή. And in particular the closest resemblance is seen between the longer narrative parables of the Gospels and the parables of the Talmud.

CHAPTER IV

THE EVANGELISTS AND PARABOLIC TEACHING

Having in the last chapter dealt with the Gospel parables themselves, we now turn to their setting in the Gospels. Both direct mention of the parabolic method of teaching, and also incidental references, provide considerable material whereby one can judge of the reasons for adopting this method. After many centuries of partial misinterpretation of this material a drastic step was taken in 1888 by Jülicher who asserted that the Gospels gave evidence of a two-fold purpose of parabolic teaching: the true purpose as it existed in the mind of Jesus, and a false mistaken idea of His purpose as it existed in the imagination of the evangelists. Jesus, he said, had used parables so as to make His teaching plainer. That He should have done so follows really from the character of Jesus who came to reveal things to men, but it is also supported by incidental remarks in the Gospels. But he asserted that the evangelists did not understand this, but believed that Jesus told His parables as esoteric mysteries only to be explained afterwards to the inner circle of disciples, and as intended to remain unintelligible to the crowd. The disciples, he said, looked upon the parables as allegories which convey no meaning at all until they are explained, while in reality they are similitudes which are self-explanatory. These opinions of the evangelists might be gathered from the words put into our Lord's mouth in answer to the disciples' question about the parables, and also from the presence of allegorical explanations of the parables of the Sower and the Tares. Following the assertion that allegory was necessarily mystifying, Jülicher proceeded to cut out as unauthentic these allegorical explanations and to prove that our Lord did not use allegory at all. All allegorical explanations, and every suggestion that our Lord used parables with the purpose of blinding and stupefying His hearers must then be due to disciples and evangelists who invented them in accordance with the tendencies of thought existing in the early Church. A theory of such boldness, backed by a weight of solid learning, was bound to be welcomed with admiration as a relief from the confused haze of opinions about parabolic teaching that held the ground until about that time. There was much in common between this theory of a sharp division between our Lord and the early exponents of the Gospel, and the theory of the Tübingen school of a sharp division between a Petrine and a Pauline party in the early Church. The theory of the Tübingen school has been rejected by everyone as essentially untrue, and yet it marked a forward step in criticism. It remains to be seen whether history will give a similar verdict on Jülicher's bold theory.

One wonders whether Jülicher ever stopped to ask himself how disciples, who had learned something about the kingdom of Heaven from parables spoken in the presence of the multitude and which received no further explanation in private, could ever have reached the extraordinary opinion that the purpose of this particular kind of teaching was to conceal the truth. But without resting too much on such subjective arguments it is better to weigh carefully the arguments for the Jülicher-theory. The previous chapters have attempted to prove that his fundamental conception of the different nature and purpose of allegory and similitude is incorrect; and further that specimens of pure allegory, and traits of allegory in similitudes, are found attributed to our Lord apart from the explanations of the Sower and the Tares. Even if this attempt be found to be successful, there remain yet the express remarks on the purpose of parable-teaching which will seem to many to be conclusive in favour of Jülicher's point of view. Few people, using the R.V., will dare to disagree with Jülicher after reading Mc. iv. 11, 12 "And He said unto them, Unto you is given the mystery of the kingdom of God; but unto them that are without, all things are done in parables: that seeing they may see and not

perceive; and hearing they may hear and not understand; lest haply they should turn again, and it should
be forgiven them." If any more is needed, the argument
is then clinched by referring to Mc. iv. 34 "and without
a parable spake He not unto them: but privately to
His own disciples He expounded all things." The
following attempt to obtain the true meaning of these
passages by paying due regard to grammar may appear
laboured. But when much depends on a few words,
words must be given their true value.

It will be noticed first of all that those who ask
about the parables (Mc. iv. 10) are not just the Twelve
specially selected by our Lord, but οἱ περὶ αὐτὸν σὺν
τοῖς δώδεκα. It is this larger band of men who have
come of their own accord because of their interest, and
not merely twelve specially favoured, who are told that
to them is given the mystery of the kingdom of God.
S. Matthew explains this further: these men evinced
an interest in the kingdom, and therefore it was given
them to know more about it than those who showed no
interest, "to you it is given to know the mysteries of
the kingdom of Heaven, but to them it is not given;
for whosoever hath, to him shall be given, and he shall
have abundance; but whosoever hath not, even what he
hath shall be taken from him" (Mt. xiii. 11, 12).

According to S. Mark after our Lord had told these
interested few that the mystery of the kingdom was
theirs, He went on ἐκείνοις δὲ τοῖς ἔξω ἐν παραβολαῖς

(τὰ) πάντα γίνεται. The usual interpretation of this
treats it as if the parables were spoken exclusively to
the multitude, and were of no value to the inner circle
of disciples. The R.V. translates it "but unto them
that are without all things are done in parables." It is
true that 'do' in some senses of the word can be used
to represent some senses of the word γίνομαι. There
are however other senses in which it cannot be used,
and certainly in any case it is a poor translation because
ambiguous. The word γίνομαι has the root sense of
'becoming' or 'coming into being.' From this root
sense it branches off into many subsidiary senses. It is
only necessary here to consider such senses as might be
applied to the case in point.

(1) It is used in the sense of 'coming to pass,'
'taking place,' e.g. Heb. vii. 12 νόμου μετάθεσις γίνεται,
Lc. ii. 2 αὕτη ἀπογραφὴ πρώτη ἐγένετο, Mc. xiv. 4
ἡ ἀπώλεια...γέγονεν, Acts xxv. 26 τῆς ἀνακρίσεως
γενομένης.

(2) It is used in the sense of 'being made,' e.g.
Acts xix. 26 οὐκ εἰσὶν θεοὶ οἱ διὰ χειρῶν γινόμενοι, or
of miracles 'being performed' or 'being wrought,' e.g.
Mc. vi. 2 αἱ δυνάμεις...διὰ τῶν χειρῶν αὐτοῦ γινόμεναι,
Lc. iv. 23 ὅσα ἠκούσαμεν γενόμενα εἰς τὴν Καφαρναούμ.
In these cases the thought is not merely of action
('doing') but of creative power.

(3) It is used of the fulfilment, of a wish Mt. vi. 10,
xxvi. 42 γενηθήτω τὸ θέλημά σου, and so Acts xxi. 14;

of a command Lc. xiv. 22 γέγονεν ὃ ἐπέταξας; of a request Lc. xxiii. 24 γενέσθαι τὸ αἴτημα αὐτῶν; or of a prophecy 1 Cor. xv. 54 τότε γενήσεται ὁ λόγος ὁ γεγραμμένος, Acts xxvi. 6 τῆς...ἐπαγγελίας γενομένης ὑπὸ τοῦ θεοῦ. Here again it is something more than 'doing,' it is 'fulfilling.'

Hence it seems that full justice is not being done to γίνεται if it is taken in the restricted sense of 'doing' which might have been expressed by ποιεῖται or λέγεται[1]. The inceptive idea of 'becoming' or at least of 'coming to pass' must be recognised.

There are fairly frequent cases in the N.T. where γίνομαι is used in close connexion with εἰς or ἐν. There is a close similarity in the meaning and they must both be dealt with here:

(1) Acts v. 36 ἐγένοντο εἰς οὐδέν, Jno. xvi. 20 ἡ λύπη ὑμῶν εἰς χαρὰν γενήσεται, Apoc. viii. 11 καὶ ἐγένετο τὸ τρίτον τῶν ὑδάτων εἰς ἄψινθον[2], Mt. xxi. 42 ἐγενήθη εἰς κεφαλὴν γωνίας, Lc. xiii. 19 ἐγένετο εἰς δένδρον, etc. Compare also 1 Regn. x. 12 διὰ τοῦτο ἐγενήθη εἰς παραβολήν, Ἡ καὶ Σαοὺλ ἐν προφήταις; In German it is expressed accurately and literally "zu

---

[1] An early scribe seems to have missed the grammatical subtlety of γίνεται ἐν, but observed that γίνεται was not the proper word to use for the 'utterance' of parables, and hence altered to λέγεται. So D 28 64 124 2ᵖᵉ a b c ff₂ g₁ i q.

[2] Winer-Moulton, p. 229 (ed. 1882), mentions these first three cases and shows that the construction is not merely Hebraic (= ל היה) as it is used in other Greek writers.

etwas werden," that is "to become (or be changed
into) something."

(2) Lc. xxii. 44 γενόμενος ἐν ἀγωνίᾳ, Acts xii. 11
ἐν ἑαυτῷ γενόμενος, Acts xxii. 17 γενέσθαι με ἐν
ἐκστάσει, Rom. xvi. 7 γέγοναν ἐν Χριστῷ, 2 Cor. iii. 7
ἡ διακονία...ἐγενήθη ἐν δόξῃ, Phil. ii. 7 ἐν ὁμοιώματι
ἀνθρώπων γενόμενος, 1 Thess. ii. 5 οὔτε γάρ ποτε ἐν
λόγῳ κολακίας ἐγενήθημεν, 1 Tim. ii. 14 ἐν παραβάσει
γέγονεν, Apoc. i. 10, iv. 2 ἐγενόμην ἐν πνεύματι. The
meaning is a state or condition into which someone or
something becomes. Just as ἐν is used with verbs of
motion to express the idea of rest and continuance
succeeding the motion[1] so here ἐν expresses the continuance of the state, while γίνομαι expresses its
inception. Although in some cases in the N.T. εἰς and
ἐν are beginning to be confused[2], in all or most of these
cases with γίνομαι the distinction is clear—with εἰς the
emphasis is on the change to a new state or condition,
with ἐν the emphasis is on the continuance in that state.
The εἰς and the ἐν following γίνομαι in Lc. iv. 23 and
1 Cor. ix. 15 are not closely connected with the verb,
but form additional prepositional clauses qualifying the
meaning of the verb. In a similar way, in the case
before us Holtzmann[3] and B. Weiss[4] connect the verb

---

[1] Winer-Moulton, p. 514 ; Grimm and Thayer, s.v. ἐν I. 7.
[2] J. H. Moulton, *Prolegomena*, p. 63.
[3] *Hand-Commentar*, Bd. I. Abt. I. p. 129.
[4] *Meyers Kommentar* (B. Weiss), ad Mc. iv. 11.

rather with the recipient than with the state or condition. They both translate "das Alles zu Teil wird,"
"everything falls to the lot" of those without in parables.
γίνομαι certainly can have this meaning as in Mt. xviii.
12, but in face of the many examples given above where
ἐν is used in close connexion with γίνομαι it is better
to connect them here. The meaning then will be that
for those without everything becomes parabolic, with
the further thought that everything remains parabolic,
i.e. they hear only the story and think nothing of the
eternal reality which the story was meant to make
clear. We can imagine one of "those who were without"
going home to his friends and saying "He told us that
a grain of mustard seed is the smallest of seeds, and
grows into a very large tree," and forgetting to say that
the growth of the kingdom of God was similar.

But if this was the result, that many turned away
nothing bettered, shall we not still think that S. Mark
believed in the blinding and stupefying hypothesis from
what follows—ἵνα βλέποντες βλέπωσιν καὶ μὴ ἴδωσιν
κ.τ.λ. ? If our Lord is actually made to say that the
reason for the teaching becoming parabolic to those
without was an eternal purpose that they should not
see however much they tried, then we cannot acquit
S. Mark of believing in the blinding hypothesis. The
question is partly one of grammar and partly of point
of view. To begin with we must remember that we
are dealing with a quotation. It is taken with some

freedom from the LXX of Isai. vi. 9, 10. There the
words are sent to the people from God by Isaiah as a
warning of the punishment that is coming upon them.
Yet no one would take them there literally to mean
that the people must utterly fail to understand, for if so
the sending of Isaiah to them was to no purpose. It is
equally futile here to suppose that the quotation of the
text means that try how they would the common people
would learn nothing from the parables. So far it is a
reductio ad absurdum. But how then is the quotation
to be taken? The most decisive word is ἵνα, because
that has always been taken to imply a purpose or
design. In classical Greek that is so. In the Κοινή
it is generally so, but the force of the word has weakened,
and there are some who would even go so far as to allow
it on occasion a purely ecbatic meaning. Sanday and
Headlam on Rom. xi. 11 translate μὴ ἔπταισαν ἵνα
πέσωσι ; by " have they stumbled so as to fall ? " They
say " ἵνα expresses the contemplated result," and after
a special note on the subject of the use of ἵνα add " we
cannot here any more than elsewhere read in a Divine
purpose where it is neither implied nor expressed,
merely for the sake of defending an arbitrary grammatical rule." Following such a lead as this, and that
of J. H. Moulton[1], we would almost dare to take ἵνα
here as ecbatic, meaning that the result of choosing
to remain without was that the teaching remained

[1] *Prolegomena*, p. 206 sq.

parabolic, and further that that resulted in blindness. But there is a half-way position supported by Grimm and Thayer for those who do not dare to go so far[1]: "in many passages where ἵνα has seemed to interpreters to be used ἐκβατικῶς, the sacred writers follow the dictate of piety, which bids us trace all events back to God as their author, and to refer them to God's purposes." This is presumably the same as what Evans calls 'subjectively ecbatic.' In the case before us it makes little difference which view we take, the subjectively or the purely ecbatic. A similar passage is Jno. xix. 28 ἵνα τελειωθῇ ἡ γραφή, λέγει· διψῶ. The purpose if any is the eternal purpose of God, and has nothing to do with the immediate individual purpose. The earliest commentator on this passage in S. Mark is S. Matthew, and he carefully removes any possibility of a telic interpretation by substituting ὅτι for ἵνα. The very most that could be got out of S. Matthew's ὅτι is that the people were blind because it was prophesied of them that they would be—but prophecy does not influence a man's actions although it may foresee them. These much debated verses then, Mc. iv. 11, 12, mean just this: that to those who are interested is given the mystery of the kingdom, but the uninterested cannot get beyond the picture, and they have thus condemned themselves, as the prophet had foreseen, to the darkness of ignorance. With such an interpretation in our minds

[1] s.v. ἵνα II. 3.

we turn with different feelings from before to Mc. iv.
33, 34. These two verses do not now give us opposing
views as Jülicher thought. "With many such parables
spake He the word to them as they were able to hear
it." It was difficult to learn about the kingdom of
Heaven, but He taught them by parables so as to make
it as easy as possible, and gave them just as much as
they could understand. "And without parable He did
not speak to them" because it was so much easier for
simple minds when He used parabolic speech. But
still He had only touched the fringe of the subject, and
those who were interested would have many questions
to ask, and they would come and ask Him, and every
one of their questions was answered for them so clearly
that the evangelist can scarcely be accused of exag-
gerating when he adds "and privately to His special
disciples He explained everything."

A short survey of some other passages will show
that the purpose of our Lord and the opinion of the
disciples, as we have traced them in the foregoing
passages, are reflected throughout the Gospels. Our
Lord's purpose of giving instruction to those who felt
the need of it, while those who imagined that they had
sufficient wisdom should go away empty, is clearly
given in the cry of jubilation Mt. xi. 25, 26, Lc. x. 21
"I thank thee, O Father, Lord of heaven and earth, that
thou hast hid these things from the wise and understanding and hast revealed them unto babes; yea,

Father, for so it became well-pleasing in thy sight." It is the same principle that appears in Mt. xiii. 12 already quoted, which the evangelist definitely refers to the purpose of parabolic teaching "for whosoever hath, to him shall be given, and he shall have abundance; but whosoever hath not, even what he hath shall be taken from him." The same principle is extended by S. Paul to the whole preaching of the gospel. The evil spirit that has gained the mastery in those who are perishing prevents them from hearing: 2 Cor. iv. 3, 4 "But and if our gospel is veiled, it is veiled in them that are perishing; in whom the god of this world hath blinded the minds of the unbelieving, that the light of the gospel of the glory of Christ, who is the image of God, should not dawn upon them." Mc. xiii. 28, followed by Mt. xxiv. 32, acknowledges that parables are intended to give instruction, when he quotes our Lord's words "from the fig tree learn the parable"; and Mc. iv. 2 admits the same fact by saying "He taught them many things in parables." Nor was this kind of teaching reserved for the crowd, while a simpler clearer method was employed for teaching the disciples, for we are told in Lc. xvi. 1 that our Lord spoke the parable of the Unjust Steward to the disciples, and in Lc. xii. 41 S. Peter asks whether the foregoing parable on watchfulness applies to all as well as to themselves. S. Matthew has also arranged the parables of the Treasure, the Pearl and the Net as if they were given privately to the

disciples at the same time as the explanation of the
Tares; and after these parables there is the significant
conclusion (Mt. xiii. 51) "Have ye understood all these
things? They say to Him, Yes." By quoting this the
evangelist admits that these three parables were intelligible although only the last had any sort of definite
'explanation.' It is scarcely fanciful to see in the
similitude, which follows in verse 52, of the scribe who
has become a disciple of the kingdom, a reference to
the method of parabolic instruction which links up the
old that is already known with the new that is to be
taught. S. Mark further quotes our Lord as definitely
repudiating the idea of anything being hidden or being
created secret in order to remain hidden, iv. 22
"for there is nothing hid, save that it should be mani-
fested; neither was anything made secret, but that it
should come to light[1]." In fine the only reasons why
things remain unintelligible are either that the hearers
take no interest, or that the subject itself is intrinsically
difficult. This latter is seen in other cases, where no
parables are used, for instance Lc. ix. 43–45 "He said
to His disciples, Let these words sink into your ears;
for the Son of Man is going to be betrayed into the

---

[1] Holtzmann, *Hand-Commentar*, ad loc., speaks of this as
"die Versicherung, dass die Wahrheit nicht zum Zweck der
Veheimlichung mitgetheilt werde, sondern zur weiteren Ver-
breitung da sei, wie das Licht da ist, um seine Strahlen so weit
als möglich zu senden."

hands of men. But they understood not this saying, and it was concealed from them, that they should not (or 'did not') perceive it." It was not then the Lord's purpose to use parables in order to conceal His message from some, nor did the disciples and evangelists so construe His purpose. If the foregoing pages be accepted there is no evidence for the theory that the disciples and evangelists misunderstood Jesus' purpose.

Further, it will be seen that since the 'explanations' of the parables of the Sower and the Tares were given in the absence of the multitude, the parables alone without the explanation must have been capable of giving instruction. If they had not been, it would have been a mockery of the common people to speak to them in that way. We shall see that the parables were capable of imparting some information about the kingdom of God; but some of the hearers were not content with this; to them the kingdom of God was such a foreign idea that to learn even the simplest lesson about it was difficult; the difficulty was intrinsic in the subject; these more interested hearers then gathered round the Lord, and He told them something more about the subject. Let us take first the parable of the Tares, Mt. xiii. 24-30. It starts "The kingdom of Heaven is likened unto a man sowing good seed in his field." In accordance with the general practice, as we have seen already, this introduction means that the condition of affairs in the kingdom of Heaven is similar

to the condition in the story. The hearer would then
have to consider, from what he already knew of the
kingdom, just where the parallel lay. Now there is
one point about the story of which he could not miss
the application : the harvest means a judgment by God.
It is in fact an allegorical trait in the story, which is
there just because the idea of God's judgment as a
harvest was a current metaphor. Here are some examples of it : Mal. iv. 1 "and all the proud and all that
work wickedness shall be stubble, and the day that
cometh shall burn them up," Jer. li. 33 "The daughter
of Babylon is like a threshing-floor at the time when it
is trodden ; yet a little while and the time of harvest
shall come for her," Joel iii. 12, 13 "there will I sit to
judge all the nations round about. Put ye in the sickle
for the harvest is ripe," Hosea vi. 11 " Also, O Judah,
there is a harvest appointed for thee, when I bring
again the captivity of my people." With this idea of
the judgment in his mind, the hearer, who tried to
compare the story with the kingdom of Heaven, would
probably arrive at the fact that the kingdom contains
good and evil until their separation at the judgment.
Here is a certain amount of teaching which anyone
fairly well acquainted with the Old Testament would
gain at once. But the disciples naturally wanted to
know more about the subject, and so they came to
Jesus. His answer, Mt. xiii. 37–43, may be said to
take the form of a further parable. This parable has

traits both of similitude and allegory. It is certainly allegorical to say that the tares are the sons of the Wicked One, because both tares and the wicked share the property of being undesirable. At the same time verses 40, 41 are certainly similitude, "therefore just as the tares are gathered together and burnt in the fire, so shall it be at the end of the world; the Son of Man shall send forth His angels and gather together out of His kingdom all things that cause stumbling and them that do iniquity." Looked at in this light these verses appear not so much an 'explanation' of the original parable, as a new parable (part similitude, part allegory) giving additional information on the same subject. There is nothing in this half similitude half allegory essentially different from many other parables of our Lord, except the mere fact that it takes as its text, so to speak, a parable already spoken. It is in fact still parable, and needs still the attentive ear, just like the rest of His teaching. Therefore it ends "He that hath ears, let him hear."

A similar treatment is accorded the parable of the Sower, Mc. iv. 2-9 and parallels in S. Matthew and S. Luke. Here the hearers are not told in so many words that the story is compared with the state of affairs in the kingdom of Heaven, but they knew that our Lord was preaching about the kingdom, and therefore the context told them where to look for a comparison. It was, one would think, sufficiently obvious that the intended

comparison lay in the varying success of the preaching
of the kingdom among different conditions. The hearers
would no doubt recall such a passage as Isai. lv. 10, 11
"For as the rain cometh down and the snow from
heaven, and returneth not thither but watereth the
earth, and maketh it bring forth and bud, and giveth
seed to the sower and bread to the eater; so shall my
word be that goeth forth out of my mouth: it shall not
return unto me void, but it shall accomplish that which
I please, and it shall prosper in the thing whereto
I sent it." That quotation is not exactly parallel with
the story of the Sower, where the thing sent forth is
the seed and not the rain, but the attention is similarly
directed to the resultant fruitfulness. Fruitfulness is a
common metaphor for success; and whether the parable
of the Sower contained in the first place any slight
allegorical traits or not, it is fairly certain that it was
capable of conveying a certain amount of instruction
about the kingdom. Then we have, as with the Tares,
an 'explanation' which gives further instruction by
making fresh parables out of the parable. It says in
effect "as thorns choke the growing corn, so do riches
and cares destroy the growing faith; as the seedling
growing on almost bare rock has no stability, so have
men no stability if their faith is not well grounded,
and so on." Justice is not done to this passage if it is
regarded as a mere allegorising of the original parable.
In fact it has been observed by some commentators

that it is remarkably poor allegory to substitute the devil for the birds of the air. In actual fact it does not make that substitution, but simply compares the bird's pecking up of the grain off the ground with the devil's snatching the word that has been newly received in the heart. The outward form of these verses, which at first sight looks like mere allegorising, can be described, like such a form of expression as "the kingdom of Heaven is like a man that is a merchant[1]," as merely due to *Inconcinnität*.

Those who have regarded these 'explanations' as mere allegorical treatments of the parables have denied their genuineness. But in one important point the passages themselves give evidence of their authenticity: the thought of the 'explanation' is an expansion of the thought of the original parable, along the same lines. When we meet with real allegorical interpretations by later hands, such as those that see Christ in the Good Samaritan, mercy and grace in the oil and wine, and that busy themselves with the interpretation of the robe, the ring and the shoes given to the Prodigal Son, the new thoughts are out of all connexion with the original parable. However useful such methods may be to the preacher they generally betray themselves as later accretions because the ideas thus suggested are put into the parable regardless of the parable's original

[1] e.g. Fiebig, *op. cit.* pp. 24, 34. Compare Jülicher, 2 Teil, p. 581. See p. 22 supra.

meaning. This was indeed the general method of allegorical interpretation. Jerome could even by this method get from the Song of Songs a proof of the advantage of virginity and a condemnation of second marriage. The so-called explanations of the Sower and the Tares on the other hand simply develop to a greater extent the ideas already in the parable. When compared with allegorical interpretations by Christian Fathers, the nature of these passages gives a strong presumption in favour of their genuineness. Even a modern writer causes surprise if he is able to bring out of a parable fresh ideas that are consistent with the original meaning of the parable: Jülicher[1] can only ascribe to a "healthy tactfulness" the fact that Stockmeyer "where he explains individual traits, gives them a meaning that Jesus could have accepted." Our experience scarcely warrants us to expect to find in a disciple of the first century sufficient "healthy tactfulness" to have composed the explanations of the Sower and the Tares. The demonstration that these passages are not mere allegory, and that even pure allegory does not necessarily serve to blind and to stupefy the hearers, has broken down the argument that we must here see the work of a later hand; and from an examination of the contents of the passages we even have a positive presumption that they are by the same hand as the original parables.

[1] 1 Teil, p. 316.

CHAPTER V

THE FOURTH GOSPEL

It is admitted on all hands that there is a distinct difference between the Synoptic Gospels and the Fourth. Christ cannot have spoken as He is represented in the Fourth Gospel if He spoke as in the Synoptic Gospels. S. John's Gospel must give us the life and words of our Lord, not as they were in actual temporal fact, but as they were seen to be in eternal reality by the devoted eyes of an early disciple. While admitting all this, one must feel that the difference between the earlier Evangelists and the later one has been pushed too far. Very noteworthy is this in dealing with the parables and figurative speech. It is commonly asserted that while the Synoptists make our Lord speak similitudes, the author of the Fourth Gospel makes Him speak in allegory, in fact the whole Fourth Gospel is regarded as one great allegory. Loisy says[1]: "Allegory is the characteristic trait of the Johannine teaching. It reigns even in the narratives, which are profound symbols whose secret the author only half-opens for a

[1] *Le quatrième Évangile*, 1903, p. 75.

moment at a time; it reigns too in the discourse, in which the Christ speaks continually a figurative language, of double meaning, which the Evangelist himself supposes to have been unintelligible for those who heard it. Thus the whole Fourth Gospel is nothing but a great theological and mystical allegory, a work of learned speculation which has nothing in common as far as form with the preaching of the historic Christ." Jülicher referring only to the figurative speech, goes nearly as far when he says[1], "The result of our investigation is this: what the Synoptists call παραβολή is a kind of figurative speech which is almost entirely lacking in the Fourth Gospel. The παροιμίαι of S. John are in the smallest degree related to the Synoptic παραβολαί." These views have not however been universally accepted, e.g. Spitta[2] says, "It is incorrect when it is asserted that the Synoptic parables are wanting in S. John's Gospel, and that in the place of the παραβολή stands the παροιμία, which is allegory. The difference of parable and allegory does not lie in the Greek terms, which are both used in the LXX to represent the Hebrew מָשָׁל, without it being possible to substantiate a difference of meaning." In the particular case of the παροιμία of the Shepherd, which has been so often described as an allegory, we have an equally strong denial from B. Weiss[3], "When

---

[1] 1 Teil, p. 117.   [2] *Z. nt. W.* 1909, Heft 2, p. 108.
[3] *Meyers Kommentar*, ad Jno. x. 6.

Meyer etc. assert that the foregoing figurative speech is no parable but an allegory because it does not tell a story, that comes from a perfectly arbitrary definition of the nature of a parable."

The evidence of the Fourth Gospel is very important to us. If it were true that the first Evangelists thought of our Lord's parables as mere allegories, and imagined His purpose to be the hiding of the truth, and if further these views were most commonly held throughout the history of the Church, we should expect to find them in S. John's Gospel. We should expect to find allegories rather than similitudes, and perhaps an expressed purpose that our Lord spoke in figurative speech to conceal His meaning. The object of this chapter is to show that we find the exact opposite, namely that the figurative speech is not mere allegory and that the purpose of Christ's method of speech is expressly declared to be in order to give instruction.

As we have found elsewhere, the figurative speech in this Gospel is not all of one kind. Perhaps we should notice first such sentences as xiii. 30 ἦν δὲ νύξ and xiii. 10 ὁ λελουμένος οὐκ ἔχει χρείαν [εἰ μὴ τοὺς πόδας] νίψασθαι, where the meaning on the face of it is plain and straightforward, but in which general consent has traced a metaphor. It is probably such underlying metaphors (if we are right in supposing that they were intended) which have given this Gospel its reputation as one great allegory.

Next, there are several short similitudes. xvi. 21, 22,
which compares the sorrow followed by joy of a woman
in travail with the present sorrow and future joy of the
disciples, is admitted by Jülicher[1] to be a similitude,
although he doubts its genuineness because of its lack
of demonstrative power. From some of the examples
of similitudes given in Chapter I it will have been seen
that they do not necessarily, as he supposed, exist in order
to bring out some *Urteil.* At any rate, genuine or not,
it is a similitude, and at present we are chiefly concerned not with the sources of the Fourth Gospel, but
with the opinions of its author. A second similitude is
xii. 24, 25, "Except a grain of wheat fall into the earth
and die, it abideth by itself alone, but if it die it beareth
much fruit. He that loveth his life loseth it, and he
that hateth his life in this world shall keep it unto life
eternal." It is sufficiently clear that the first of these
two verses is a picture of the second, without there
being a definite word of comparison. Another similitude
is put into the mouth of John the Baptist, iii. 28, 29,
"Ye yourselves bear me witness that I said I am not
the Christ, but that I am sent before Him. He that
hath the bride is the bridegroom; but the friend of the
bridegroom, which standeth and heareth him, rejoiceth
greatly because of the bridegroom's voice: this my joy
therefore is fulfilled." That this cannot be an allegory
is shown by the fact that there is no one to whom the

[1] 1 Teil, p. 116.

bride could refer. The similitude lies in the comparison of the relationship between bridegroom and friend with that of Christ and John the Baptist.

Besides these shorter similitudes there are two longer and more complicated ones of the Vine and the Shepherd. Commonly they have been regarded as allegories, but it would seem better to look on them as similitudes which have been worked up in much the same way that the 'explanations' of the Sower and Tares work up the thoughts of those parables. Spitta sees that the παροιμία of the Shepherd has received the same treatment as the Sower and Tares, although he is led to regard that treatment in both cases as the allegorising work of a later hand[1].

The parable of the Vine, xv. 1–6, bears plainly the mark of similitude, verse 4 "As the branch cannot bear fruit of itself, except it abide in the vine; so neither can ye, except ye abide in me." On the other hand there is what looks at first sight like allegory, verse 5 "I am the vine, ye are the branches." If it is allegory we must ask, In what way is Christ like a vine, and in what way are the disciples like branches, except in the one particular of their relationship to one another? If the only likeness is this relationship, it is not the

[1] *Z. nt. W.*, 1909, Heft 1, "Wie bei einigen synoptischen Gleichnissen das Nichtverstehen der Bilderrede Anlass wird zu einer allegorisierenden Ausdeutung (vgl. Mt. xiii. 36, Lc. viii. 9) so auch hier."

elements that are being compared but the relationship
between them. In fact, in spite of the form, it is
nothing more than similitude, and we have again the
familiar *Inconcinnität* which appears in the Synoptic
parables when the kingdom of Heaven is said to be
like a merchant, or a grain of mustard seed. Now the
various thoughts that are brought out, of the relationship
between Christ and His disciples as being similar to
the relationship between a vine and its branches, are
built up into the parable round this one comparison.
B. Weiss thinks that there was an original parable
spoken by our Lord that has suffered this working over
by the Evangelist[1], but admits the impossibility of
separating the strands. For our present purpose the
only point of importance is that the author of the
Gospel represented our Lord as speaking in this way,
and that this way was not an unintelligible, mystic
manner of speech, but similitude with at most some
traits of allegory, not differing essentially from the
parables of the Synoptic Gospels. There is of course
a difference between the Johannine and the Synoptic

---

[1] *Meyers Kommentar*, ad Jno. xv. 8 "Bei der Johanneischen
Art der Wiedergabe der Christusreden ist es natürlich ganz
unmöglich, den ursprünglichen Wortlaut der Parabel und ihrer
Anwendung herzustellen, aber gerade hier tritt es aufs klarste
hervor, dass wir hier nicht eine vom Evangelisten geschaffene
Allegorie haben, sondern dass durch seine Auffassung und
Deutung noch die Erinnerung an echte Jesusworte deutlich
hervorblickt."

parables, but it is not in their essential nature; it is rather that S. John favours a discursive style, e.g. in inserting verse 3 "ye are already clean because of the word which I spake unto you," instead of sharply separating the parable from the rest of the discourse.

The parable of the Shepherd in chapter x. presents similar problems, but the whole discourse is more complicated.   Here again allegory is now-a-days denied. B. Weiss says it cannot be allegory because many traits have no allegorical meaning[1], and Spitta agrees with him[2]. Wellhausen, Schwartz and Spitta all try to explain the changes in thought and language, that occur in this parable, as due to the work of different hands. For this purpose the first two writers feel obliged to prefer the reading of the Sahidic version in verse 7 ($\pi o\iota\mu\acute{\eta}\nu$ for $\theta\acute{\upsilon}\rho a$), and all three writers disagree as to the division into what is primary and what is secondary. Such divisions into different strands should properly be, not the first resort of criticism, but the last resort when it is found impossible to get an intelligible view of the passage as the work of one man.   In the preceding chapter we read of the healing of the blind man, and

[1] *Meyers Kommentar*, ad Jno. x. 6 "Dagegen ist das Vorige schon darum keine Allegorie, weil (wie Meyer selbst zugiebt) viele Züge des Bildes gar nicht für die Deutung bestimmt, kein einzige aber um der Deutung willen erfunden ist, vielmehr das zur bildlichen Darstellung bestimmte Naturverhältnis rein als solches geschildert wird."

[2] *Z. nt. W.*, 1909, Heft 1.

down to verse 34 is brought out the thought of how he
rejects the Pharisees and clings to Jesus who has healed
him. Verses 35–41 bring out further the judgment
that the blind man is given sight because he knew his
blindness, but that the Pharisees became blind because
they thought they saw. x. 1–5 now takes up the earlier
thread and explains that as sheep can recognise their
true shepherd, so can God's people recognise their true
teacher. The parable is now complete, just as the
parable of the Sower was complete before the 'explanation' was given. But the discourse proceeds with a
series of 'explanations,' so to speak making fresh
parables out of the parable[1]. In each the behaviour of
the Pharisees is referred to that of the false shepherd.
The first of these passages is in verses 7–10. Here the
idea is given of the falsity of the Pharisees because like
false shepherds, thieves and robbers, they have not
approached in the right way. Their relationship to
Christ is like the relationship of a thief to the door of
the fold; their relationship to Christ is also like that
of a thief to a true shepherd. In an allegory it would
be impossible to make Christ at once a door and a
shepherd, but in a similitude both comparisons are
legitimate. Surprise is shown by commentators at
verse 8 "All that came before me are thieves and robbers,"
but this may easily be taken as a slight exaggeration,

----

[1] Cf. supra, p. 62.

meaning that many teachers were false, and not as condemning the whole Old Testament. This whole passage is connected with the parable of verses 1–5 by means of the behaviour of the robbers which is compared with that of the Pharisees. This connexion is more tangible than the one that Spitta finds with ix. 35–41 In the same way the behaviour of the Pharisees is compared in the next passage, verses 11–13, with that of false shepherds with their flocks in the field. This second passage is also naturally connected with the first by verse 9 which speaks of a man going out to find pasture for the sheep. Here in the second passage is the comparison of the shepherds when the sheep are on their pasture. Christ Himself is typical of all good teachers, so that He can contrast Himself with the Pharisees as the good shepherd as opposed to the hireling. That Christ is speaking of Himself as typical teacher is seen by the reference first to *men* going out to find pasture, and then to Himself doing the same work—"I came that they may have life." Hence verses 9 and 10 lead on naturally to verse 11 "I am the good shepherd." The remaining verses 14–18 deal with one chief characteristic, the self-sacrifice, of Christ the typical teacher or pastor, and in these verses the figurative form of speech is gradually laid down, until we find that it has become literal and straightforward. It is the strange way in which the similitudes in this chapter fit into one another, and then gradually fade

away into normal speech, that lent colour to the notion
that we were dealing with allegory.

There are yet three passages to be considered, which
also bear on their face the stamp of allegory. The first
is a long discourse, vi. 32–58, centring round the sentence
"I am the bread of life"; the other two are short
sayings, viii. 12 "I am the light of the world" and
xi. 25 "I am the resurrection and the life." Are these
in fact allegory, or in what sense are they to be taken?
We must first look at the discourse of chapter vi. more
closely. It falls clearly into four sections, separated
from one another by the interruptions and murmurings
of the Jews, and a progress of thought may be traced
throughout: (1) verses 32, 33 introduce the subject
with the sentence "the bread of God is that which
cometh down out of Heaven," (2) verses 35–40 contain
the assertions "I am the bread of life" and "I am come
down from Heaven." The Jews murmur, and (3) in
verses 43–51 Jesus explains that since they are all
taught of God their bread must come from Heaven, and
that since He is come from Heaven He must therefore
be the bread of life. This argument is followed by a
new assertion "the bread that I will give is my Flesh"
which produces a fresh striving of the Jews. Their
difficulty is explained in (4) verses 53–58 which contain
the two great statements, "except ye eat the Flesh of
the Son of Man and drink His Blood, ye have not life
in yourselves," and "he that eateth my Flesh and

drinketh my Blood abideth in me and I in him." Now throughout this it may be said in some degree to be a metaphor to speak of "bread of life" meaning the spiritual aid to spiritual life; but beyond this it is difficult to see either allegory or similitude; for one cannot say "the bread that I will give is like my Flesh," or "represents my Flesh," or "my Flesh represents the bread," or "I am like the bread of life." Nor is it easier in the other two passages mentioned: "I am the light of the world," viii. 12, might possibly be turned into the form of a similitude by a complete rearrangement, e.g. "As the Sun lights the world so do I light your hearts," but no amount of wrenching can twist xi. 25 "I am the resurrection and the life" into any sort of allegory or similitude. In what sense then is the copulative verb to be taken in these passages? The only conclusion possible is that it means "IS really, essentially, mystically." In the real, essential, mystic sense it is true to describe Christ as the bread of life. In the same sense it is true to say that His Flesh offered on the Cross is the bread that gives life to the world. The same meaning of the word 'is' can alone give sense in the Synoptists' account of the Institution of the Eucharist[1]: the bread, which to all appearances is merely bread, in a mystical, essential and real sense is the Body of Christ. In the same sense He who was the first-fruits of the Resurrection, and in whom all

[1] Mc. xiv. 22 and ||s.

others rise, can Himself be called the resurrection and the life. In the same sense too He that lighteth every man can call Himself the light of the world, as He had been already called in the prologue of the Gospel, i. 9. Thus we find the author of the Fourth Gospel in these passages using not so much the figurative forms of similitude and allegory as the philosophical thought of ideas and essences.

We come now to the explicit utterances of the Fourth Gospel on the subject of Jesus' method of teaching. First we turn naturally to xii. 35–41, a passage which contains that same quotation from Isaiah which the Synoptists used in this connexion. In verse 35 our Lord tells the multitude that the light is at present with them, but they must use it now lest darkness overtake them. Evidently our Lord was teaching in clear language, and warned the people to accept the teaching while they might, or else they would find themselves unable to grasp it. In fact this did happen to many, and Jesus was hidden (or hid Himself) from them, verse 36. So it came about, as Isaiah had said, that they did not believe the report, that their eyes were blinded and their hearts hardened. The point of importance in this passage is the fact that the judgment was brought upon the multitude by their own obstinacy, although they had the chance of seeing the light. It is to be noticed that according to the Gospels our Lord spoke in parables throughout His ministry, and therefore parables must have been a method of giving light or instruction. The next passage is xii. 46–48 where the same thought is continued that Christ came a light into the world. Here His preaching is specially mentioned: "If any man hear my sayings and keep them not, I judge him not; for I came not to judge the world, but to save the world;...the word that I spake, the same shall judge him in the last day," from which it is obvious that our Lord's method of teaching was capable of imparting instruction, or else it could not judge those that failed to be instructed. In xiv. 22–24 our Lord is represented as repudiating definitely the suggestion of an esoteric teaching. Judas asked "Lord, what is come to pass that thou wilt manifest thyself unto us, and not unto the world?" Jesus answered "If a man love me he will keep my word; and my Father will love him, and we will come unto him and make our abode with him. He that loveth me not keepeth not my words." In other words the only thing necessary in order to be able to comprehend His teaching was love. In xvi. 25–33 the question is again raised. Our Lord contrasts His present teaching in parables (παροιμίαι) with His future teaching plainly (παρρησία). At present they were unable to understand when He spoke without parables as is shown by what immediately follows: He spoke of His coming from the Father and His going back to the Father. The disciples thought that now since He was not using parables they understood much better, and joyfully they replied (verse 29) " Lo, now speakest thou plainly and speakest no parable; now know we...; by this we believe...." But Jesus knew well that they could not yet properly understand such plain speech, and so with a note of sorrow He replied " Do ye now believe ? behold, the hour cometh, yea is come, that ye shall be scattered every man to his own and shall leave me alone." In fact this speaking without parable was not so much ἐν παρρησίᾳ as the disciples thought. They had understood better when he used parables. But now verse 33 brings a word of comfort; though they have understood so little yet He has taught them enough to give them peace, "these things I have spoken to you that in me ye might have peace." The climax comes in xviii. 20. Christ is arraigned before the High Priest, the chief of the sacred hierarchy of Israel. The High Priest asks Him solemnly about His disciples and His teaching. Now if at any moment one expects a careful and exact answer. "Jesus answered him, I have spoken openly (παρρησίᾳ) to the world...and in secret spake I nothing."

It is inconceivable that the Evangelist who recorded all these sayings, and doubtless, as most now-a-days believe, put them into his own words so as to record the thoughts rather than the mere words, believed in the theory that our Lord spoke in parables in order to blind and stupefy His hearers.

CHAPTER VI

CRITICISM OF THE PARABLES

The principles of the use of parables by our Lord
here laid down have found expression from time to time
in the history of the Church. Men whose own work
was largely teaching could scarcely fail to see the object
of using figurative speech. If the purpose of parables
was to conceal the truth from sinners by way of
judgment on them, we should have expected to have
found a change of attitude on the part of our Lord, so
that He only spoke parables in the latter part of His
ministry after the Jews had rejected His plain teaching.
Lagrange[1] says that to his knowledge Chrysostom is
the only Father who notes any change of attitude on
the part of Christ. But even Chrysostom does not
suppose that the parables could not be understood, for
he says εἰ γὰρ μὴ ἐβούλετο αὐτοὺς ἀκοῦσαι καὶ σωθῆναι,
σιγῆσαι ἔδει, οὐχὶ ἐν παραβολαῖς λέγειν· νῦν δὲ αὐτῷ
τούτῳ κινεῖ αὐτούς, τῷ συσκιασμένα λέγειν. Again he

---

[1] *Revue Biblique Internationale*, 1910, p. 7 note. For some
of the quotations that follow I am also indebted to Lagrange.

says[1] Ἐπειδὴ γὰρ αἰνιγματωδῶς ἔμελλε διαλέγεσθαι, διανίστησι τὴν διάνοιαν τῶν ἀκουόντων πρῶτον διὰ τῆς παραβολῆς. Διὰ τοῦτο καὶ ἕτερος εὐαγγελιστής φησιν, ὅτι ἐπετίμησεν αὐτοῖς, ὅτι οὐ νοοῦσι, λέγων· Πῶς οὐκ ἔγνωτε τὴν παραβολήν; Οὐ διὰ τοῦτο δὲ μόνον ἐν παραβολαῖς φθέγγεται, ἀλλ᾽ ἵνα καὶ ἐμφαντικώτερον τὸν λόγον ποιήσῃ, καὶ πλείονα τὴν μνήμην ἐνθῇ, καὶ ὑπ᾽ ὄψιν ἀγάγῃ τὰ πράγματα. Οὕτω καὶ οἱ προφῆται ποιοῦσι. Thomas Aquinas is very clear on the point, e.g. he says[2] "Est autem naturale homini ut per sensibilia ad intelligibilia ueniat; quia omnis nostra cognitio a sensu initium habet. Unde conuenienter in sacra Scriptura traduntur nobis spiritualia sub metaphoris corporalium....Sacra, doctrina utitur metaphoris propter necessitatem et utilitatem." At the same time he recognised that the disciples were fitted to receive more truth than the common people; there are three ways, he says[3], in which doctrine can be hidden, "uno modo quantum ad intentionem docentis, qui intendit suam doctrinam non manifestare multis, sed magis occultare...quod in Christo locum non habuit ex cuius persona dicitur (*Sap.* VII. 13) quam sine fictione didici, et sine inuidia communico, et honestatem illius non abscondo....Tertio modo aliqua doctrina est in occulto quantum ad modum docendi. Et sic Christus quaedam

---

[1] Migne, *P. G.* LVII. col. 467.
[2] *Summa Theol.* Pars I. Qu. I. Art. 9.
[3] *Summa Theol.* Pars III. Qu. XLII. Art. 3.

turbis loquebatur in occulto, parabolis utens ad an-
nuntianda spiritualia mysteria, ad quae capienda non
erant idonei uel digni. Et tamen melius erat eis uel
sic, sub tegumento parabolarum, spiritualium doctrinam
audire, quam omnino ea priuari. Harum tamen parabolarum apertam et nudam ueritatem Dominus
discipulis exponebat, per quos deueniret ad alios, qui
essent idonei." There are of course in the history of
the Church opinions which differ from these. For
instance Maldonatus, admitting that his opinion is not
generally held, says "Non dubito...ideo Christum hoc
quidem loco parabolis usum fuisse, non ut auditores
melius intellegerent, sed ut, qui credere nolebant diserte,
aperteque loquenti, loquentem per parabolas, et obscure,
etiam si maxime uellent, intellegere non possent."
And besides such direct statements as this, there is the
large mass of commentary on the parables which treats
them as if containing deeper mysteries than lie on the
surface. This last phenomenon, although it has been
made so much of, weighs with us very little when we
remember that not the parables only, but all scripture,
Old and New Testament, was subjected to this treatment. Even when writers speak expressly of the
enigmatic nature of parables it is well to remember
that such language was used of the contents of the
whole Bible.

Coming to modern thought we find that until the
last two or three years criticism of the parables was at

a standstill, because men stood spell-bound by the
fascination of Jülicher's theory.   Questions for instance
of genuineness have been left almost untouched because
men's hands were tied by the theory that made them
condemn unheard the 'explanations' of the Sower and
the Tares.   At last criticism could no longer be bound.
Even Weinel who tries to follow faithfully in the steps
of Jülicher has admitted that the theory went too far
although he still believes it essentially correct[1].   Others
have not been so cautious.   Fiebig's criticism is
smashing, if not altogether wise, while other writers
have begun to use the parables critically and to forget
the bonds of the theory.   These writers know that the
parables constituted an important part of our Lord's
teaching, and therefore for the sake of the substance of
that teaching, and perhaps with little care for theories
about methods of teaching, they demand of the parables
what they have to teach.   In order to do this they
must either break or despise the bonds of the theory
which has held them in.   Then the investigation
widens: it is no longer a piece of work separate from
other studies, but deals with questions of the genuineness and nature of all the teaching attributed to our
Lord.   As it thus leaves the narrower basis of criticism
of the parables *qua* parables, it is proposed in this
concluding chapter only to point out in broad outline
the questions now before us.

[1] See *Z. nt. W.* 1912, Heft 2, p. 118.

There are questions first of the genuineness of the parables and their higher criticism. Much of this is not new, for instance it has generally been felt that the parables of the Talents Mt. xxv. 14 and the Pounds Lc. xix. 11 although differing in various points go back to a common original. Apart from the minor differences of the value of the coin and the number given to each servant, there are additions in both Evangelists. S. Matthew adds the mention of the casting out of the unprofitable servant, while S. Luke mentions the embassage of the citizens, and their punishment. S. Matthew's addition can easily be understood as an embellisment which the parable would get through being preached; but S. Luke's addition is no ordinary embellishment, the thought expressed by it being obviously out of context. One is almost obliged to look on it as a part of another parable which has been joined on none too skilfully. The differences between the parables of the Supper as told in Mt. xxii. 1 and Lc. xiv. 16 are of the same order. The addition in Mt. xxii. 11 about the man without a wedding garment, like S. Luke's addition to the parable of the Pounds, seems altogether out of context. The thought does not dovetail into the rest of the parable like that of the Sower and its 'explanation.' It is therefore to be presumed that it has come from a distinct parable. It must clearly be understood that this separation is not demanded because similitudes cannot bear more than one point of

comparison, but because this fresh comparison is quite
foreign to the thought of the other comparisons. Besides
this addition there are other differences; e.g. while, according to S. Matthew, the servants are sent out only
once to fetch in the poor, according to S. Luke they went
out twice, the second time into the highways and hedges.
Prof. Denney sees in this addition a fresh comparison
suggested by missionary expansion[1]. To be contrasted
with S. Luke's addition to the parable of the Pounds,
and S. Matthew's addition to the parable of the Supper,
is the addition about mammon, Lc. xvi. 9, to the parable
of the Unjust Steward. Undoubtedly it starts a fresh
train of thought, but it is not an unskilful addition like
the other two. It rather bears a relation to the way in
which the 'explanation' of the parable of the Sower
has been shown to be connected with the parable itself.
The addition is congruous with what has gone before.
The parable had taught wisdom and forethought, and
this is a particular case of it—the wise use of money.
If the unskilfulness of those other additions, and the
absence of any inner connexion of thought with what
had gone before, inclined us to think of the additions
as made by the Evangelist, the skilfulness and subtle
connexion of thought in this case would rather incline
us to think of the addition about mammon having been
made by our Lord. Higher criticism has ever been too
ready with its scissors, as seems to have been the case

[1] *Expositor*, Aug. 1911, " Criticism and the Parables."

in the Old Testament. Is it not possible that a more
scientific higher criticism will resist the natural desire to
cut off this passage and the 'explanations' of the Sower
and the Tares as later accretions? There is no doubt
that the parables must have undergone changes between leaving Jesus' lips and being transcribed by the
Evangelists. This we have seen in the cases of the
Supper and the Talents. But this is not to declare
that any parables have so far departed from their
original form that the parables of the Tares and of the
Seed growing of itself could be, as Denney suggests,
forms of one parable spoken against interference with
the course of events. We should be rather inclined on
the other hand to allow that generally speaking the
parables have not altered materially in transmission.
It stands almost to reason that being easily remembered
they would be less liable to alteration than other kinds
of sayings. It is even questionable whether we are
obliged to see the mark of a later hand in such
sentences as Mt. xxv. 21 "Enter thou into the joy of
thy lord," Mt. xxii. 6 "And the rest took his servants,
and entreated them spitefully, and slew them," and
Mt. xxv. 12 "I know you not." Even yet it is not
possible to speak the last word on the genuineness of
the parables. They must be used, together with all
other records, for the elucidation of Jesus' teaching,
and only as that investigation is carried further can it
be said with any certainty that such and such passages

are to be rejected as incongruous with His doctrine or His method of teaching. In proportion to the genuineness of the parables will their use in the quest of the historical Jesus and His teaching be fruitful and lasting.

It is mostly with regard to the instruction given on the kingdom of Heaven that modern writers look to the parables. Denney[1] for instance suggests that the reaping of the seed growing secretly is to be taken into account as well as the rest of the parable, so that the parable teaches the gradual growth and also the catastrophic crisis of the kingdom. In a recent discussion between Prof. Burkitt and Mr Streeter on the kingdom as represented in the parables[2], Burkitt speaks rightly of the spiritual meaning of knowing the mystery of the kingdom: "It really is the fact that we must know 'the mystery of the kingdom of God' if we are to understand the parables of the kingdom. It is the fact that otherwise we see and do not perceive, we hear and do not understand." One cannot help feeling that when people realise that to understand the parables of the kingdom it is necessary to have something of the character which is fitted for the kingdom, less will be heard of the blinding and stupefying hypothesis. The inner circle of disciples understood the parables, and Jesus' other preaching as well, better

[1] *Expositor*, Sept. 1911.
[2] *Interpreter*, Jan., Apr. and July, 1911.

than the outsiders, not because of some privileged position, but because their natures were more akin to the nature of the kingdom. It all comes back, like many another question, to a matter of character. Whether the kingdom had come or was yet to come when Jesus spoke has troubled many. Streeter takes ἔφθασεν ἐφ' ὑμᾶς in Mt. xii. 28 as "has already come," Burkitt as a reality on the point of arriving. If by the latter he means something like the moment at which the cotyledons of the seedling are just showing above ground, it is likely that the solution of the problem will be found not far off. At any rate it is in a careful study of the parables that men will learn most about the great work which Christ came to perform—the founding of His kingdom. Loisy in a moment of inspiration[1] has seen how in the mind of the Fourth Evangelist it was fitting that He who came to bring Heaven to Earth should use parables: "Throughout the length of His ministry Jesus used this figurative language, which explains heavenly things by means of earthly things....This form of teaching was suitable to the earthly condition of the Incarnate Word." It is refreshing to find that not the contents alone, but even the form, of the parables can testify to the character of Jesus Christ.

[1] *Le quatrième Évangile*, p. 792.

INDEX OF SCRIPTURE PASSAGES

Printed in the United States
By Bookmasters